DOING THE
WAINWRIGHTS

214 FELLS, FOUR SEASONS
AND A CARAVAN

OR

Where there's a wimp
there's a way

by STEVE LARKIN

Know The Score Books Limited
118 Alcester Road
Studley, Warwickshire, B80 7NT
Tel: 01527 454482 Fax: 01527 452183
info@knowthescorebooks.com
www.knowthescorebooks.com

A CIP catalogue record is available for this book from the British Library

ISBN: 978-1-905449-34-7

Jacket Design by Lisa David
Book Designed and Edited by Andy Searle

Photographs courtesy of the author, Jen Larkin and Malcolm Reid

Printed and bound in Great Britain by
William Clowes Ltd, Beccles, Suffolk

To my wife Jen and to Marjorie Harper, each of whom in their respective ways made possible the venture which this book describes

Contents

Acknowledgements

It will be immediately apparent to anyone reading this book that I owe a great deal to Wainwright's Pictorial Guide to the Lakeland Fells. These volumes were my starting-point when planning this exercise and they kept me company throughout. I have drawn on them frequently, particularly in the appendix where so often I could do no better than refer the reader to them for substantial parts of the routes I took. So thank you, AW. Thanks are also due to Frances Lincoln Ltd, the current publisher of the Pictorial Guide, for permission to quote from it.

My wife Jen has been enormously supportive of this whole undertaking. For that support, as well as for the perspicacity of her comments on drafts of this book, I am deeply grateful.

My thanks to Simon Lowe of Know The Score Books for believing in this book and publishing it and to Andy Searle and Lisa David respectively for designing the interior and the exterior of the book so beautifully; to Eric Robson for kindly agreeing to write a foreword; and to Malcolm Reid, who, along with Derek Blair, accompanied me up Blencathra, for permitting me to use photographs he took on that occasion.

Save on that very last excursion, doing the Wainwrights has been, as I felt it had to be, a solitary experience. However, I was always conscious of the fact that many people were supporting me indirectly by their sponsorship. My thanks to all who contributed to the fund-raising side of this exercise and thereby to my motivation.

And finally, my heart-felt thanks to all those members of the NHS through whose hands I passed in the years immediately preceding the one described in this book. Without their care and professionalism, I would have had no tale to tell in the first place. Indeed, I may quite possibly not have been here.

Foreword

Not the old pains in the chest malarkey again. Doesn't everyone who reaches a 'certain age' start worrying about them? But for Steve Larkin they were real rather than hypochondriac. Half way up Blencathra he had an intimation of being dead on arrival.

Then he went on to do the Wainwrights. Not the same day, you understand. There was a bit of medical intervention in the meantime. But, and this is the important "but", he dragged himself back from that moment when lesser men decide to take to the metaphorical bath chair and did the mountains.

And thank goodness he did because his book is an inspiration. (Sound of men of a certain age shoving book back onto shelf while muttering 'sod off, I don't want to be told what to do by another do-gooder'.)

But don't.

I know, I know. We get lots of that from everybody from the Department of Health to the makers of tasteless margarine. But the difference with this book is that it's real and rooted in personal experience rather than limp-wristed theory.

It took Steve 64 expeditions to do all 214 fells. And this is a man with a heart condition, remember. But more important than the ticking off of mountains is Steve's ability to capture the moment; to bring those expeditions to life on the page. He's almost as good as his doctor.

If you've read this far, book an appointment at the cash desk and get a copy.

Eric Robson
Chairman, The Wainwright Society

Chapter One

Getting Started

IT IS 27 JULY 2002 and I am about to nip up to the top of Blencathra before we - myself, my wife Jen and our younger daughter Kate - leave the Lake District and head back home. I had hoped to climb it on my sixtieth birthday (25 July), but the weather put paid to that. Now, however, it is a lovely afternoon with good visibility, so off I go.

It is an excellent way to celebrate turning sixty, but it is also something of a warm-up for an altogether more ambitious scheme. I am planning to do the Wainwrights, in other words to climb all two hundred and fourteen fells covered by Wainwright in his wonderful series A Pictorial Guide to the Lakeland Fells. And I plan to do them in the space of just one year, from 1 August 2002 to 31 July 2003. It will be quite a challenge, as I am less fit now than I have ever been. The daily run has long since bitten the dust, a victim of anno domini and a long succession of injuries. So this project is in part an attempt to reverse the process of physical decline. But it is also an opportunity to raise funds for a local charity, M.E. North-East, in which we as a family have a direct interest - more about that later. The summer issue of Focus, M.E. North-East's quarterly magazine, has already announced this scheme of mine, including the start and finish dates, so it is now in the public domain and I really am committed.

I have decided to climb Blencathra by the Doddick Fell route - steep but less fearsome than the more direct Hall's Fell ascent which, wimp that I am, I have never had the courage to tackle. I walk around the foot of Scales Fell, cross Scaley Beck, clamber up the rock on the far side and am onto Doddick Fell. This is where the climb proper starts and it starts steeply. There is a family up ahead, progressing quite slowly, and I am rapidly gaining on them when I become aware of a discomfort in the centre of my chest. I am blowing hard, so I stop for a breather. Everything settles down and I press on once more. After a hundred metres or so the discomfort comes back, but I don't want to keep stopping and starting, particularly with this family just ahead of me, so I ignore it. It gets worse. It's not just discomfort now, it's pain and I have to stop. Fortunately, the family has settled down on a grassy knoll below me and I feel free to take my time over this.

I sit down. I have never experienced anything like it before and am not sure what I should do. However, now that I have stopped the pain has gone and I really do want to climb Blencathra, not least to find out if an ache in my heel, which has been niggling for a week or so, has finally cleared up. So on I go.

The path continues to rise steeply and I find that I am forced to stop more and more frequently. This is getting worrying and I envisage the possibility of abandoning the walk. By now, though, I am more than halfway up the ridge and going back seems almost as problematic as going on. Besides, once at the top of Doddick Fell, instead of continuing to the summit of Blencathra I can take the gentle descent by Scales Fell back to the road. That seems like a good plan, so I carry on, stopping as and when necessary. By going more slowly, I find that the pain takes longer to come back and is less bothersome when it does. By the time I reach the top of Doddick Fell, I have more or less come to terms with it.

Now I have to decide. Do I turn left to the summit of Blencathra or right to Scales Fell and the road? I know that while I was struggling up the ridge there had been no question in my mind: I was going to turn back. But now that I am here, the summit of Blencathra is not that far away, the gradients involved are much less steep and the pain really has eased. It seems a shame to miss the opportunity on such a lovely day, so I turn left. In doing so, I am aware that I have reneged on my earlier decision and that my choice is perhaps not an entirely wise one. I fudge the issue by walking slowly and, somewhat to my surprise, reach the summit without any further discomfort. My decision, it seems, is vindicated, but getting to the top gives me no great pleasure. I am too preoccupied by what is, or might be, going on in my chest and so I do not linger, conscious of the fact that it is a long way back down to the road.

Down is the key word, though. The effort will be minimal, so there is no reason why I should get any more pain. I pass the top of Doddick Fell without any problem and am descending the grassy slopes of Scales Fell before the pain comes back. I stop. This time I am not just worried, I am scared. For the first time in my life I feel mortal. I am out on the fells, at least three quarters of an hour away from car and family, with no means of communication available to me, and I have chest pains which will not go away even though I am walking downhill. I try walking more slowly. It makes no difference. The only plus in all this is that the pain is less acute than it was on the way up. It doesn't go away, but at least I can keep walking, which is what I do. After what seems like an eternity I reach the road. Now that I am on the level and walking effortlessly the pain at last subsides and before long I am back with my wife and daughter. I truly am a lucky man!

At home, my G.P. diagnoses a cardiac problem and puts me on medication. It is obvious that all fell-walking will have to wait till the results of various tests are known. In other words, my project is kaiboshed before it has even started. Still, it is open to me to postpone my start date till, say, September or October rather than calling the whole thing off. At least, I hope it is.

That hope is soon dashed. Even quite short walks from home bring on the chest pain and my G.P. puts me on further medication. He also advises me to avoid doing anything remotely strenuous. In due course I have an exercise test on a treadmill and that too induces the pain. The consultant suspects angina and wants to do a further, more precise test to establish how many arteries are affected. The catch is that there is a three-month waiting-list. My thoughts of starting on the fells in a month or two bite the dust and I contact M.E. North-East to tell them that I have had to shelve the whole project.

Meanwhile, Jen and I have been debating whether to go ahead with the holiday we have booked at Grange-over-Sands. After considerable heart-searching in more senses than one, we decide we will go. We set off the day after the exercise test but, once there, I find that the angina is triggered more and more frequently and becomes progressively more acute. Less than a week after our arrival, I end up in a high-dependency coronary care unit in Barrow-in-Furness General Hospital. At first it seems that I have had a heart attack, but subsequent tests suggest that I haven't. Even so, I remain in hospital for five days. Once back on my feet, I soon discover that three hundred yards on level ground is the most I can manage to walk. Slowly.

This state of affairs persists throughout September and the first half of October, at which point I am admitted to hospital for an angiogram. This reveals that the main artery delivering blood to the wall of the heart is completely blocked. No wonder I have been having problems. The specialist carrying out the procedure tells me that the chances of opening up the artery are fifty/fifty - it all depends on how long it has been blocked. I fervently hope that he can succeed, as the alternative does not bear thinking about. The procedure continues and, to my immense relief, is entirely successful. The artery is opened and a stent inserted to keep it that way. The contrast in the blood supply to this part of the heart wall - virtually non-existent before the procedure and in full flow afterwards - is captured for me by the specialist on two adjacent screens. Where before all had been a largely featureless, grey expanse, now there is what looks like a great river with a host of tributaries carrying blood to every corner. I cannot put into words the relief and gratitude I feel. Once again I am a truly lucky man.

Now all I have to do is recover confidence and fitness, a gradual process in both cases. By mid-November I am back walking in the Lake District, albeit at low level, but without experiencing any ill effects. Subsequent progress is briefly interrupted by an unrelated minor operation, but on 26 May 2003 I climb to the top of Blencathra for the first time since that fateful day the previous July. I really am back on track. Thereafter, I get across to the Lakes regularly, build up the length of my walks and, best of all, experience no problems whatever with my heart. I start thinking once more about the fell-walking project. Might I perhaps make a start on it next spring? There seems no reason why not, but fate has other things in store.

In February 2004, after blood tests and a biopsy, I get confirmation that I have prostate cancer. On current evidence it is operable and I have the choice between surgery and radiotherapy. I opt for surgery and once again forget about the Wainwrights. At the end of August I have a radical prostatectomy which, in the light of subsequent tests, appears to have been completely successful, though I will be monitored for several years to make sure. Yet again I have cause to count my blessings.

By mid-October I can just about manage short, low-level walks in the Lake District but the tops are beyond me and remain that way for some time. In November, sitting in the car near Grasmere after a gentle, lakeside walk, I look across to Helm Crag and find myself wondering if I will ever manage to climb it again - or any other fell, for that matter. But by February

Doing the Wainwrights

2005 I am able to climb some of the easier fells and my thoughts turn once more to doing the Wainwrights. I talk it over with Jen, wondering if the project is still feasible. The more we talk the less feasible it seems and yet I feel deeply reluctant to wave it goodbye. It is undeniably a challenge and I am by no means convinced that I can do it. But then, if I knew now, with absolute certainty, that I could do it, it wouldn't be a challenge, would it? And as the professional adventurer John Ridgway once put it, "Nothing worth having is easily achieved."

Besides, I hate the feeling of shrinking horizons. In the past I have had to accept that my running days are over. I now have to accept that taking pills and carrying a spray with me for angina attacks are an inescapable part of life. I am beginning to come to terms with the fact that, given the heart disease, certain projects with which I had vaguely flirted, like the tour of Mont Blanc, may be beyond me. But the idea that I can no longer contemplate doing the Wainwrights is something I simply cannot accept, at any rate not without cast-iron proof. I resolve to use my next visit to the Lakes as a test to see how I get on over four days of slightly more ambitious walking. Meanwhile, I step up my work-rate in the gym where I have been attempting to get into some sort of shape over the last few months.

In early March 2005, blessed with favourable weather, I manage thirteen modest fells in four days without experiencing any ill effects. In the light of that, I decide to go for it. I'll get started on the Wainwrights on April the first, before some new problem has a chance to raise its head. I contact M.E. North-East once again and also the British Heart Foundation, to which I feel a debt of gratitude after my recent experiences. I also do an interview for my local paper, the Hexham Courant, with a view to raising public interest in what I am attempting. It just so happens that the next issue is due out on the day I plan to start.

Getting Started

And sure enough, come the day there is an article and a photograph. Once more the project is back in the public domain. All I have to do is do it!

Chapter Two

The First Four Days

IT IS APRIL THE FIRST 2005 and I am pulling on my boots at the foot of a grassy slope. This is the moment I have been waiting for since the summer of 2002 and I feel a tingle of excitement. Yet it has to be said that I am starting less with a bang than a whimper. The plan, announced in the Hexham Courant, had been to begin with the Fairfield horseshoe, a beefy hike which would have given me no less than eight fells on my first outing. But, as the saying goes, man proposes and God disposes. April the first turns out to be a dismal day with a lot of low cloud and misty rain and the forecast holds out the prospect of little improvement.

"So what?" says a voice inside my head, when I first register what the day is like. "This is the Lake District, not the Costa del Sol. You just have to take the weather as you find it and make the best of it. Otherwise it's not a year you're going to need for this project of yours, it's a decade!"

While one part of me acknowledges the wisdom of this point of view, I remain unswayed by it. The problem is that at heart I am and always have been a fair-weather walker. I like to see where I am going and I want glorious views in return for my efforts on those laborious ascents. Far from being a thoroughbred fellsman, out in all weathers, enjoying the challenge of everything that nature can throw at me, I am more of a tourist, camera at the ready. I am also, it has to be said, a pretty dodgy navigator, particularly in mist. Consequently, on this first day of April I elect to tackle not the sublime, in the shape of the Fairfield horseshoe, but the ridiculous, which in this case proves to be Binsey.

Binsey, I should explain, is a little, round hill standing alone in the extreme north-west corner of the Lake District. It is a pleasant hill offering fine views in good weather, but in no sense is it demanding. Indeed a stroll up its gentle, grassy slopes to the summit takes me all of fifteen minutes, so it is hardly in the same league as Fairfield. Nevertheless I feel a sense of exhilaration every step of the way, and particularly on reaching the top and touching both the Ordnance Survey column and the highest stone on the tumulus alongside it. One down and two hundred and thirteen to go! I really am embarked on this adventure.

Having walked up the eastern slope, I decide to make a round of it and descend northwards to High Ireby. Wainwright speaks of the excellent views over the coastal plain and the Solway Firth from this part of the route, but I have to take his word for it since the 'view' is today concealed by an impenetrable haze.

Back at the car I cannot help feeling that, even for a wimp like me, this start to my campaign is altogether too much of a whimper. Encouraged by the fact that the nearest and northernmost fells are clear of the clouds that shroud their larger neighbours, I decide to try and add to my tally for the day. After a short drive and an early lunch, I set off from Longlands for the little gorge called Trusmadoor (lovely name).

There it occurs to me belatedly that I have not informed Jen of this unscheduled extension to my route. I had rung home before setting off to let her know that my destination was Binsey, but I had better keep her up to date with my intentions. Fortunately the mobile phone which I now carry with me at all times has a good signal and I ring up. My daughter Kate answers. "I'm climbing Great Cockup," I tell her. There is a silence at the other end. "Great Cockup," I repeat. After a pause, she says: "This is an April fool, isn't it?"

I can see her point. One part of me wonders if climbing Great Cockup on April the first doesn't just about sum up this whole undertaking. I suppress the thought and explain that yes, Great Cockup really is the name of the fell I am climbing and that it will lead to others, whose names I go on to recite. By the time I have finished, I think I have convinced her.

Climbing out of Trusmadoor onto Great Cockup is a simple matter, but finding the true summit of the fell is not, for it has a relatively flat top with three widely separated cairns, any one of which can seem higher than the other two, depending on your perspective. To be on the safe side, I touch the top of all three - a routine I will repeat on any fell where the true summit is in doubt. With no view to be had, it is back down to Trusmadoor and up over Meal Fell to Great Sca Fell, my highest point of the day. All this walking is relatively easy, the fells here being rounded and grassy, more like the Cheviots than the Lake District, and I start to feel that the five extra fells I have set my sights on for the day are as good as in the bag.

I head off confidently across a trackless expanse of tussocky grass to my next objective, Brae Fell, only to find on arrival that it isn't Brae Fell at all. The tiny cairn bears no resemblance whatever to the one illustrated by Wainwright, and now that I am here I can see clearly that Brae Fell lies in a quite different direction. Telling myself, not for the first time in my life, that I really should make more use of my compass, I dig out my map and find that I am on Yard Steel, a prominent point, to be sure, but not one of Wainwright's fell-tops. So it's back over the hummocks to Little Sca Fell and from there, by an excellent path which I should have found first time around, to Brae Fell. I am still clear of the heavy cloud which obscures everything just south of my patch and so I have no problem in reaching Longlands Fell, my final objective for the day. By now my legs are making clear that all they want to do is stop, but with six fells in the bag that's fine by me. This first day, I tell myself, has not been such a whimper after all.

The weather next day proves to be much better. The cloud is higher and the forecast good, so I set out to do the Fairfield horseshoe. I have decided to do it clockwise, starting with Nab Scar. No sooner have I left the main Ambleside-Grasmere road than the path begins to climb very steeply indeed. Wainwright describes this route as "steep in its middle reaches" but it has me blowing hard all the way. After fifteen minutes I start shedding clothing and soon find myself caught between the contradictory demands of excessive body heat and public decency. It's the dilemma every walker knows: you are too hot so you shed clothes, which makes your pack heavier, which makes you hotter still, so you shed more clothes…

I reach the top of Nab Scar after fifty minutes' very hard work. The views from here are evidently first-rate but it is such a hazy day that all I can do is read Wainwright and savour them vicariously. I climb on over Heron Pike and Great Rigg, at which point I can see the cloud feeding in from the valleys below, as well as other, heavier cloud blowing in from the sea, all of which makes me feel a bit anxious. Fairfield in cloud is a real teaser, as I know all too well, having once come off it in a hurry aiming for Patterdale, only to find myself in Ambleside. I can still remember the pain of toiling over the Kirkstone pass at the end of a long day.

Sure enough, as I climb up towards the summit of Fairfield it disappears in cloud. I proceed cautiously, with Wainwright in one hand and compass in the other. I know that routes from at least four different directions converge here and that, if I am not to get hopelessly confused, I must remember clearly the direction from which I have approached the summit (just west of south) and the direction I need to take off it (east then south-east).

Doing the Wainwrights

A fellow-climber is having his lunch on the top and I ask him which of the numerous cairns he thinks marks the summit (I will visit it in due course). Not unreasonably, he concludes from my question that I need more substantial guidance and, on learning of my proposed route, proceeds to point me in exactly the opposite direction to the one I require. Had I followed his instructions, I would have found myself scrambling over the terrifying Cofa Pike en route for Patterdale when, this time, I am actually aiming for Ambleside. Fortunately, I disregard his directions. Sticking to my compass and my Wainwright I find myself, when the sun comes out shortly afterwards, bang on course for my next target, Hart Crag. There is a moral here.

From Hart Crag, the route is a long and gradual descent to Ambleside, taking in three more fells - Dove Crag, High Pike and Low Pike - along the way. Under clear skies I enjoy every minute of it, but by the time I reach the road my knees are complaining and my legs suddenly turn to jelly after all that downhill work. Getting them to operate normally on the flat is a major exercise, but the car is parked near Rydal, so there is nothing for it but to stumble back along the road. I fall into the car six and a half hours after I set off, shattered and with blisters on both heels, but feeling hugely pleased. In two days I have climbed fourteen fells. Only two hundred to go! At this rate I'll have them all done by... The ensuing mental calculations are rudely interrupted by the insistent messages coming from my legs which tell me there is no way they can keep this up day after day. Perhaps they have a point. I decide then and there that tomorrow will be easy.

I wake next day to better weather still, with all tops clear and a good forecast. I am sorely tempted to change plans and capitalize on the good visibility in order to tackle more of the major fells. However my legs still feel heavy, so I stick to my plans and drive west to Loweswater village, from where I intend to climb just two modest fells. My first target is Mellbreak, which rises dramatically from the shores of Crummock Water. Wainwright is most enthusiastic about it, especially if it is climbed by the direct route up the northern ridge. I have never been near this fell before, but it sounds like a splendid walk and I set off in eager anticipation. The countryside around me is beautiful, more rural than the wilder parts of the Lake District and with spring lambs in the fields adding to its attractiveness, and I come out onto the open fell feeling ready for anything. Then I see for the first time what the direct route involves - a steep and prolonged scramble over loose scree - and I know instantly that it is quite beyond me.

Never mind. Wainwright offers an easier route B so I decide to take that. It turns out to be a high-level crossing of an increasingly precipitous slope on a path that is at best narrow and at worst minuscule, and it too involves negotiating various patches of scree. I stick with it for what seems like an eternity, my eyes riveted on the path ahead of me, since any stray glance down the slope instantly causes vertigo. Eventually, with no easier ground in sight and the slope getting visibly steeper, I decide to turn back. This is far from being an easy option but, since I cannot face going on, there is nothing for it but to grit my teeth until I get back to more congenial surroundings.

In due course I find myself more or less back at square one. Now I must tackle the only option still open to me - Wainwright's route C. Will I be able to manage it or is Mellbreak going to prove beyond me? The idea that my whole scheme may be about to turn into the great cockup I had feared - and at such an early stage in the process - is too awful to contemplate. I set off with renewed determination.

The route starts off innocuously enough following the Mosedale valley, which allows me to relax once more and enjoy the surroundings. I can see now just how steep is the hillside I had been traversing and it is clear that, had I stuck with it, the remainder of the route would have been no less trying. My present path poses no such problems and when it suddenly leaves the valley and heads straight up the hillside I get stuck in and thoroughly enjoy the climb, even though there are times when it feels as if it is not far off vertical. But there is no scree beneath my feet and my eyes are fixed on the rising ground ahead of me, so there is no vertigo to contend with. When the path finally levels out, I am wholly in my element and thoroughly enjoy exploring the top, visiting both summits north and south.

Now it is time to descend. I have been trying not to think about it too much, since route C is the only descent available to me and I know just how steep it is. Curiously, it turns out to be far easier than I had imagined. For some reason I don't quite understand, going straight down the hillside like this seems not to provoke vertigo, while a level path where the ground falls away sharply on one side certainly does. Or perhaps it is sheer desperation - there is, after all, no alternative. At all events, I am soon back down by Mosedale Beck where I have a bite of lunch before tackling my second fell of the day, Hen Comb.

Like Mellbreak, Hen Comb is an unknown quantity, but it proves to be a straightforward climb over grassy slopes all the way to the top. Nevertheless, the last third of the climb is really steep and my legs are soon telling me that this is anything but an easy day for them. They have a point. Quite apart from all the to-ing and fro-ing on Mellbreak, I am climbing each of these fells from scratch. And so I learn an obvious lesson the hard way: it is not the number of fells you climb but the amount of ascent involved which determines whether a day is hard or easy.

The view from the top of Hen Comb is disappointing as the haze which has been about all day is getting thicker, so I have a quick look round and then return to the car by my outward route. Mission accomplished. I am sorely tempted to leave it at that, but I have never visited Loweswater (the lake) before and am not sure when I'll be this near again. So, after a short rest, I force my legs into action once more and walk to the far ? the lake and back. With the weather deteriorating, the w? looks slate-grey. National Trust signs warn of blue-green alga? which may be toxic and on that sobering note I return to the car. Now at last my legs can rest up in readiness for the final day.

This proves to be overcast and showery and I settle for an easy walk in the northern fells, starting from Mungrisdale. I climb Bowscale Fell by the easiest of the four routes described by Wainwright, since I know that anything more demanding will put paid at the outset to my plan of doing four fells, albeit carefully chosen ones. Once on top of Bowscale Fell, the day's climbing is to all intents and purposes over and a brisk walk takes me via Bannerdale Crags to Mungrisdale Common, where my biggest problem is finding the highest spot. Wainwright is very apologetic about this "fell" which is in fact a barely sloping, tussocky expanse. I scour it for almost fifteen minutes before locating the neat little cairn which has been erected since his time.

From here, I skirt the northern side of Blencathra whose summit is within easy reach, but I am saving that for my final fell (if I ever get that far) and plan to climb it properly, i.e. from the south, not sneak up on it from behind like this. So I cut across to Souther Fell, another whose true summit is not easy to locate. It is a very elongated fell and the temptation is to imagine that if not the southern tip then the northern one commanding a lovely view over Mungrisdale must be the summit. In fact it is neither, the highest point being set back maybe a third of a mile from the northern end. It is barely marked, there being little stone around with which to mark it, so it is easy to miss. Even though I have been up here before and have read Wainwright on the subject, I still feel unhappy about turning back at what I know is the highest point, when the northern tip, which I can see ahead of me, looks at least as high, if not higher. So to be on the safe side I tramp over to it and, sure enough, when I look

from which I have come, I can see that the

recedes. This too might be discounted as

but on my way back my legs provide

of that I am indeed climbing, however

..... the spot identified by Wainwright is without

doubt the true summit.

Having visited my four fells for the day, I make a gentle descent to the River Glenderamakin (another lovely name) and so back to Mungrisdale. Totting up the sum of my efforts over these first four days, I find that I have walked nearly forty miles and climbed over ten and a half thousand feet (3,200 metres) in notching up twenty fells. To say that I am pleased with the way things have gone is a huge understatement. I am over the moon! To be sure, my legs are extremely weary - it will take a whole week after my return home before they stop aching - but I have already completed my quota for April and I have another trip to the Lakes lined up for the end of the month.

As I sit at home sticking the first twenty red dots on a map of the Lake District, I reflect on the fact that I have managed four substantial excursions without experiencing any alarming physical symptoms and without ever getting seriously lost. Of course there is plenty of time for things to go wrong yet, but at least this first part of the process has not, after all, proved to be the Great Cockup I half expected.

Chapter Three

April

BY THE LAST WEEK of April I had well and truly recovered from my earlier exertions and was raring to go again. With another four days of walking lined up, I started this time by tackling the four most easterly of Wainwright's fells, namely Selside Pike, Branstree, Tarn Crag and Grey Crag.

It was a day of glorious sunshine, perfect for exploring an area I had never visited before. I set off from near Mardale Head, taking the Old Corpse Road by which Mardale's dead were for centuries transported over the hills to Shap for burial. The day was so lovely and my spirits so high that it never occurred to me to wonder if this choice of route was not perhaps some sort of omen. In no time at all I had splendid views back over Haweswater, where a huge flock of gulls, brilliantly white against the deep blue of the water, clamoured from a small island which they seemed to have overrun entirely. From the far side of the reservoir rose the mouth-watering ridge above Riggindale which leads directly to the summit of High Street. Wainwright calls this "the connoisseur's route up High Street" and it only took one glance for me to know that one of these days I would have to explore it.

The Old Corpse Road proved to be an excellent way onto the ridge leading up to Selside Pike, and now there were more fine views, this time over Swindale. This green valley, almost entirely enclosed by steep-sided hills and with Swindale Beck meandering the length of it, likewise cried out for further exploration, but for now I had to leave it behind me.

A simple walk over grassland with the occasional peat-hag took me from Selside Pike up to Branstree, at two thousand three hundred and thirty-nine feet (713 metres) my highest point of the day. Summits come in all shapes and sizes, but this one was decidedly an anti-climax, being no more than a few stones and the base of a trig-point on a barely rounded hill. No matter. A summit is a summit, when all is said and done, and this was one more ticked off.

From Branstree my route undulated over more grassland and peat-hags to Tarn Crag and Grey Crag, two more undistinguished summits. I thoroughly enjoyed striding out on this section of the route, pushing myself on the uphill inclines and free-wheeling on the downhill ones. It was all new territory to me and, what is more, I seemed to have it entirely to myself, apart from the sheep, that is. With the sun still shining out of a clear blue sky, I revelled in it all.

From Grey Crag I attempted to follow Wainwright's route down to Sadgill in Longsleddale, but it was far from obvious on the ground, to me at any rate, and I eventually came out at Stockdale Bridge, some two-thirds of a mile further south. By this time I was feeling pleasantly tired and paused for refreshment at a lovely spot beside the River Sprint, still a modest stream at this point despite its rather grand name. From there the walk up to Sadgill and beyond was a delight. The stone bridge at Sadgill offered another lovely stopping-point - my legs were by now quite weary - before I continued up the narrowing valley. The further I advanced the more dramatic the scenery became, as the crags on either side closed in, towering above me. What a splendid route, and here I was, almost back at my starting-point - or so I thought.

Then the track started to climb, and to climb with a vengeance: I was on my way up the Gatescarth Pass. Coming at the end of the day after nearly twelve miles' walking and around two and a half thousand feet (660 metres) of ascent, it just about finished me off. Several times when I felt that it could not possibly continue upwards it did precisely that and I began to fear that I had somehow gone astray and was in fact struggling up the adjacent Harter Fell. When finally I reached the top of the pass I sank down on a rock, utterly exhausted. Luckily I still had a little left to eat and drink and, with my energy levels slightly restored and gravity on my side, I stumbled down to Mardale Head and made my way back to the car, parked appropriately enough at the start of the Old Corpse Road. I vowed then that I would never again underestimate passes.

In planning this route I must have been so preoccupied with the fell-tops that I had regarded the pass as no more than a simple and convenient return route. After all, passes by definition go over the lowest ground, don't they? Subsequent investigation revealed that this particular pass involved a climb of about twelve hundred and fifty feet (380 metres), the equivalent of throwing in an ascent of Catbells at the end of a tiring day. I shall not repeat the mistake.

Next day the weather was still excellent and I decided that it was time to tackle some of the higher fells. I drove to Seathwaite in Borrowdale and was amazed to find literally dozens of walkers streaming along the road to the farm as if to a football match. There were even Union Jacks on display. This was not at all my cup of tea. Fortunately for me, the vast majority of walkers seemed to be heading for Scafell Pike - it was obviously going to be standing-room only up there today - and once I turned off the main highway to that ever-popular destination it was altogether more peaceful.

And what a glorious scene was spread out around me as I climbed over Allen Crags and on towards Glaramara, whose numerous tarns sparkled in the sunlight. Even though there was a haze, the views were breath-taking. I could make out patches of snow on Skiddaw eleven and a half miles away, while nearer to hand were the massive fells which constitute the heart of the Lake District - Esk Pike and Bowfell to the south, the Scafells and Great End to the west, Great Gable to the north-west, in short the Lake District at its grandest.

I took the summit of Glaramara in my stride and descended the twenty-foot rock step on the far side of it without turning a hair (I was already familiar with it), before finding a sheltered but sunny spot for lunch. Now all that remained was for me to climb Rosthwaite Fell, an altogether more modest target that I thought would take me no time at all. Wrong again! Rosthwaite Fell may be modest in height but it is extensive in area, comprising a whole range of mini-fells each with its own crags and valleys, and it has no clear path leading unerringly to the summit. I must have climbed half a dozen rocky outcrops in the belief that they were or might be the highest point before I got my first glimpse of Bessyboots, which is generally regarded as the summit. It looked far enough away to be almost a separate fell!

Once I had reached it a new problem presented itself. How was I to descend to Seathwaite? Wainwright speaks of a "straightforward" route via Comb Gill, but first I had to find it, no easy task on such a complex fell-top. If I couldn't find it - and I didn't fancy tackling the descent otherwise, for it is extremely steep - then the only alternative would be to trek back almost to the top of Glaramara, a prospect at which I quailed after all the effort I had expended in reaching Bessyboots. So off I set in search of the Comb Gill route, hoping against hope that I would find it. Whether I did or not I am still unsure, but I found a path of sorts which took me much of the way down, so that even after I managed to lose it I was still able to reach the valley floor with no real difficulty. Back at the car, I was surprised to find that this route, which was three miles shorter than the previous day's, had taken exactly the same amount of time. Rosthwaite Fell, for all its relatively modest height, requires a lot longer to negotiate than some of its more illustrious neighbours.

Next day saw me operating in the north-western fells, again under clear blue skies. As I walked along the road from Thornthwaite to the Swan Hotel, the Bishop of Barf (a prominent, painted boulder) gleamed white on the hillside above me. Its sidekick, the Clerk, is by contrast entirely inconspicuous, though I spotted it on leaving the road at the Swan and making my way up through the woods to the summit of Barf. This path must rank among the steepest in the Lake District, but the summit is a glorious spot worth every drop of sweat exuded on the way up. In particular it offers magnificent views of the Skiddaw massif, whose uppermost ridges were still lined with snow. With the hard graft of that ascent behind me I could relax for the rest of the day, as I strolled over gentle, grassy slopes to Lord's Seat, Broom Fell and Graystones, from where a steep descent took me down to Aikin Beck. Here I saw my first tadpoles of the year and spotted a buzzard circling high above me.

After improvising an ascent to the western end of Whinlatter, I walked the length of the fell. In the process, I passed over two "summits" each of which, when viewed from the other, appeared higher. Wainwright hedges his bets as to which is the true summit, but the Ordnance Survey map has no such doubts, crediting the eastern top with a height eight metres in excess of Brown How, the western one, and underlining the point by referring to it as "Whinlatter Top". Never having visited Whinlatter before, I enjoyed the walk along the lovely, level promenade it offers, with a fine view of the Skiddaw massif ahead of me. A good, clear path led down to the visitor centre in the forest, after which all I had to do was to follow another path back to Thornthwaite village.

Doing the Wainwrights

Just as I was congratulating myself on how well the walk had gone, I came upon a sign informing me that the path I wanted was closed to the public for six months. The supposedly well-marked diversion was nowhere in evidence, so I tried following a combination of forestry roads which appeared to be heading in the right direction, i.e. downwards, only to be brought back to the same footpath but half a mile further down the hill. Again a sign proclaimed the path closed to the public, but there was neither a well-marked diversion nor any obvious alternative to retracing my steps. It began to feel as though I was trapped in some gigantic forestry maze, until an elderly couple came bowling along the closed path and assured me there was no difficulty about following it down to Thornthwaite, something they had done every day for the last week. It turned out that there had been a landslip, a legacy of the January storm, which had affected the footpath, though this remained perfectly negotiable and I was soon back at the car after this latest lesson in the fallibility of the planning process.

For my final day, which like the previous three offered clear blue skies throughout, I took to the eastern fells. Starting from Patterdale, I climbed Arnison Crag, of whose existence I had been entirely unaware all these years. A short but delightful climb took me to a very satisfying, pointy summit, with fine views back over Ullswater and Place Fell. Then came a steep pull up to Birks, from where I had a clear view of my major objective for the day, Saint Sunday Crag. This I climbed obliquely, visiting Gavel Pike first. It is the lower of the fell's two summits and, with no one else about, the tranquillity was absolute as I sat watching three buzzards riding the thermals from the valley below.

On reaching the true summit, I found myself in something of a dilemma. Should I descend south-west to Deepdale Hause and hope that there was a path leading down to Grisedale Tarn or should I head north-east and go back over Birks to

Patterdale? I did not want to revisit Birks if I could avoid it, but suppose there was no path down to Grisedale Tarn, which in Wainwright's day there wasn't. I would then have to scale Cofa Pike and Fairfield in order to reach the tarn, a route I remembered, from the one and only occasion many years previously when I had followed it, as not far short of terrifying. After some heart-searching I decided to take a chance and head south-west in the knowledge that, if all else failed, I could always climb back over Saint Sunday Crag and then over Birks.

I started my descent and was almost stopped in my tracks when Cofa Pike came into view. One look at it as it reared up formidably from Deepdale Hause and I knew that my days of climbing it were over. What a blessing that Wainwright does not include it among his lakeland fells! Resisting the temptation to turn back then and there, I continued down to the Hause where to my delight I found a path, and a surprisingly good one at that, which led me all the way to Grisedale Tarn. So I was able, after all, to avoid both Cofa Pike and the need to retrace my steps. I made my way back to Patterdale by way of the Grisedale valley, getting stunning views as I went of Saint Sunday Crag on my right and the fells leading up to Helvellyn, including Striding Edge, on my left. It had been a wonderful day's walking from start to finish and my grand total of fells now stood at thirty-five, which put me almost a month ahead of schedule. What was more, I had no aches, no pains, just general fatigue. Things were looking good!

Chapter Four

Planning

IT GOES WITHOUT saying that any attempt to do the Wainwrights involves a degree of planning. I dare say there are those who have the entire campaign mapped out in advance, who know every single route they will take and when they will take it. I am not such a person. For me, planning everything down to the last detail amounts to planning the thing to death. It creates a kind of straightjacket which I instinctively resist. I like flexibility, the freedom to respond to changing circumstances. So when this project was in the planning stage my approach was far from exhaustive. I planned just about enough to get it started, after which, I told myself, I could invent it as I went along, with all the benefits that that entailed - keeping the project fresh and largely unregimented (others might prefer to call it chaotic) and giving me that room to manoeuvre in the light of experience or circumstance that I was anxious to preserve.

Given the objective of climbing all two hundred and fourteen fells in one year, I decided that I needed a monthly target, which I fixed at twenty fells. If I stuck to that, I would be finished in a shade over ten and a half months, which gave me a bit of leeway if anything went wrong.

Next I had to work out how many days I could manage in the Lake District in the space of twelve months. Initially I was thinking along the lines of one four-day spell per month, giving me a total of forty-eight days but, when I realized that

that would involve averaging almost four and a half fells a day, I reluctantly conceded that it was too demanding. It was just as well I did, since a trial four days' walking subsequently brought me just thirteen fells, by which time I was more or less on my knees. Eventually, after all sorts of combinations and permutations, I came up with the following: I would make fourteen four-day visits and three nine-day visits to the Lakes, giving me a grand total of eighty-three days, which meant that I would need to average a shade over two and a half fells per day. That, it seemed to me from the comfort of my armchair, was feasible, and so it proved on my trial outing in March.

The next step was to try and carve up the fells into not more than eighty-three routes. This I did in a very rough and ready way, taking each of the Wainwright volumes in turn and gathering the fells into what looked like logical clusters. This produced a total of sixty-eight groups of fells each of which, on the face of it, could be tackled in one day, though as I had not plotted a single route in any detail, it remained quite possible that many of these groups would need to be further sub-divided. I should probably have pursued the matter further but, telling myself that I had a comfortable margin to play with, I left the overall scheme at that. The only further planning I did was to plot half a dozen routes in some detail so that, for my first visit to the Lakes, I had a degree of choice as to where I went. To do any more planning than that was, I found, quite beyond me.

One thing I was clear about: I did not want to tackle the fells on an area by area basis, walking all the northern Wainwrights first, say, then moving on to the eastern fells and so on. I wanted to move around the Lake District in a largely random way, achieving maximum variety of terrain and scenery in the process. Indeed, I made it almost a point of honour not to walk twice in the same area during any four-day spell.

That requirement was easy enough to meet. Others were much less so. I did not want to have to repeat any climbs if I could avoid it, nor did I want to be faced by the prospect of a host of "odd-man-out" fells which I had failed to incorporate into an overall pattern and which would therefore have to be climbed singly. Given my rather piecemeal approach to planning, I suspect that there were always going to be some fells in this category. Thus the Fairfield horseshoe, while it is a splendid route and an excellent way of covering eight Wainwrights in a day, leaves intractable problems in its wake. On the western side one is left with Stone Arthur, which connects with nothing other than the fells of the Fairfield horseshoe and which must therefore be tackled as a one-off fell from Grasmere. On the eastern side Hartsop above How presents a similar problem, involving an out-and-back walk from Deepdale Park. It is true that, by continuing from Hartsop above How, one can eventually get at other fells that remain to be climbed, but in that case Hart Crag and Dove Crag have to be climbed en route and they have already been visited as part of the horseshoe.

I became aware of the problem only after I had walked the horseshoe, but even now I do not see that I could have done much about it. Any attempt to include Stone Arthur and Hartsop above How in that walk would have been foolish, for the route was already quite challenging enough. The alternative - to forget about the horseshoe and somehow tackle the east and west flanks separately - would, I am convinced, have posed more problems still. As far as I am concerned, if one or two odd-man-out fells are the price of such an excellent route as the Fairfield horseshoe, then so be it.

I suppose that, if I had planned the whole exercise more rigorously, I would have prioritised certain fells according to specific criteria and would have ensured that they could all be climbed in optimal conditions. Once again, however, I was content to plan in a much more perfunctory fashion. To be sure, I was aware that I needed good weather and, preferably, plenty of hours of daylight to tackle those fells which were either difficult of access or particularly high and exposed or unfamiliar to me. Given that I would be starting in April, it followed that ideally I should have climbed all these fells before winter set in. In practice, this was never going to be possible.

For one thing, I discovered to my surprise that at least half the Lakeland fells were completely unknown quantities as far as I was concerned. For another, my walking base, a caravan located near the foot of Blencathra, was on the north-east edge of the Lake District, so that almost all the southern and western fells were by definition difficult of access. If one then considers how many fells deserve the description 'high and exposed', it soon becomes clear that my top priority categories covered just about every fell in the Lake District. So really all I could do was try to capitalise on any good weather that came along, favouring first one category, then another in a fairly random way, but with an underlying tendency to focus on those fells most difficult of access.

In bad weather, of course, the problem is how to get any sort of walk at all. It is all very well setting off to the Lake District with six splendid routes in mind, but if you wake up to a blanket of cloud at five hundred feet and, like me, you prefer not to go on the tops in mist, then planning goes by the board and improvisation takes over. What this usually means in my case is the rapid concoction of a shortish, familiar, low-level route which, if the cloud lifts just a bit, will salvage something from the day, and I soon learned the value of having a short list of such routes to hand.

I imagine that the planning supremo, as well as having all his routes plotted in advance, will have given some thought to the significance of certain numbers. He will want fell number 1 and fell number 214 to be special of course, but others too no doubt

- numbers 50, 100, 107, 150, 200 for example. Maybe he will even aim for some kind of overall symmetry, with carefully plotted crescendos of altitude building up to each of the fells over three thousand feet, to be followed by no less carefully elaborated decrescendos. Needless to say, none of that was to be found in my haphazard way of going about things. From the moment it became clear that Binsey was to be my first fell, the significance of numbers was exploded and since then the process has been a largely random one. I suppose that, in a sense, the only really significant numbers are 1 and 214, and I knew from the outset which fell the latter would be, always assuming that I made it that far.

What emerges most clearly from the whole exercise where planning is concerned is that, no matter how much or how little you plan, there is a huge provisionality about the whole thing. The most graphic illustration of that is provided by the health problems which kept the entire venture on hold for over two and a half years. But even leaving matters of health aside, there are plenty of other factors over which you have no control and which can play havoc with your plans. The weather is the most obvious and made its presence felt from day one, since when I suspect that those days on which I actually walked the route I had planned the day before are a minority of the total. Even when I thought a particular day's walking was going according to plan, I would find myself obliged to re-think in the light of unexpected circumstances - stepping-stones across a river which turned out to be submerged, a path closed on account of a landslip, a foot-bridge which had been simply swept away or a scrambling route closed because a peregrine falcon is nesting nearby. All of which, I confess, confirms me in my view that planning is all very well, but only up to a point and provided that it is not set in stone.

Chapter Five

May

IN THE MIDDLE of May, I took the first of my nine-day spells in order to capitalise on what I hoped would be good weather and once again I was incredibly lucky, enjoying seven fine days on the trot before the rain finally arrived.

Given that my plan for the first day involved a long route over challenging terrain in an area that was completely unknown to me, it was perhaps just as well that the date - Friday the thirteenth - did not register with me till afterwards. I set off from the western end of Ennerdale Water early on a cold, clear morning. The water of the lake was a deep blue, in sharp contrast with the vibrant green of the foliage on the broad-leaved trees. Before long I had heard my first cuckoo of the year and would hear it many more times as the day progressed. It was one of those magical days when everything - sight, smell and sound - contributed to a sense of unending delight. I was carried along on a wave of elation and excitement too, particularly when I got my first glimpse of Steeple.

This was my first target and one about which I felt more than a little apprehensive, given what Wainwright has to say about it: "The east crags ... give a fine airiness to the summit and to the rocky spine of the ridge climbing out of Ennerdale to reach it." As I made my way across Ennerdale Fell and then, tentatively, up the ridge in question, I had no idea whether my nerve would hold and take me over the summit, down to whatever awaited me on the other side and then up onto Scoat Fell. Indeed, I was quite prepared to beat a retreat if, as I half suspected, I found all that "airiness" too daunting. "If in doubt, don't" was the sound advice Jen had long since instilled into me, and I found myself repeating the phrase like a mantra as I climbed ever nearer the top of Steeple.

In point of fact, the ascent proved to be no problem at all, for while the ground fell away very steeply on the eastern side, to the west there was enough of a grassy slope to make me feel comfortable as I climbed. Admittedly I stayed on the tiny summit only long enough to photograph nearby Pillar and the distant views of Scotland and the Isle of Man. This was partly because I felt very exposed there and partly because I was preoccupied by what the next section of the route might have in store for me. As it turned out, getting off the summit involved a steep but straightforward descent to the col. Here the ground fell away sharply on both sides, but I kept my eyes glued to the path and in a few moments I was across and climbing the ridge up to Scoat Fell. Fifteen minutes after leaving Steeple, I reached the summit and was able to relax once more: the most fearsome part of the journey was over.

I enjoyed the summit-cairn with the abandoned walking-boot balanced on top of it - did the owner hop back down? - then decided to take a look at the path leading from Scoat Fell to Pillar. Viewed from Steeple it had appeared excessively steep and I was prepared, if necessary, to omit Pillar this time and tackle it another day from the east. On closer inspection I decided that it was just about manageable and so it proved. After one or two slightly anxious moments involving a bit of scrambling, I arrived at the summit, which afforded me a spectacular panorama calling for yet more photographs. Then I peered gingerly over the north face down to Pillar Rock - definitely a no-go zone as far as I was concerned - before returning to Scoat Fell, from where I made an unscheduled detour south to Red Pike, for the path was so clear and the climb so easy that it seemed criminal not to do it. Then it was back to Scoat Fell once more before heading west this time to Haycock, at which point I had approached or left Scoat Fell from north, south, east and west.

The outstanding views which had been a feature of this walk all the way were still in evidence from Haycock, which offered an even clearer view of Seascale and the Isle of Man than Red Pike had done. Now all that remained was to add Caw Fell to my haul, after which I was glad to make the long descent to Ennerdale Water, for the wind had been steadily freshening during the afternoon and was now strong. I reached the car, tired but exhilarated, nine hours after setting out. I had covered sixteen miles and climbed just over four thousand feet (1,220 metres) in notching up my six fells. It really had been a wonderful day with perfect weather, stunning views - I had taken no less than eighteen photographs - and routes that had worked out without a hitch. It had also been quite a challenge both physically and mentally, but I had come through it unscathed and without once turning back. So much for Friday the thirteenth.

Saturday was a lazy day, with an easy walk over two modest fells in the north-west of the Lake District, Ling Fell and Sale Fell - the latter particularly lovely in the evening sunlight and offering a fine view over the northern part of Bassenthwaite. I would have liked to explore the Wythop valley, from which Sale Fell rises, and its adjacent woods, but I had started late and time did not allow. I needed to be up and about bright and early next day.

Come Sunday morning I was ready for another substantial effort and set off for Rosthwaite in Borrowdale. Yet again it was a perfect day, with the cuckoo calling loud and clear and bluebells in masses all the way up Stonethwaite Beck. My plan was to do a circular route starting with Ullscarf and ending with Eagle Crag, but as soon as I set eyes on the latter I knew that I wanted to start with that and resolved to reverse my route.

Doing the Wainwrights

Not only that, but I decided to climb Eagle Crag by Wainwright's more adventurous route A. For a wimp like me this was an unprecedented decision, a rush of blood to the head prompted by the sheer exhilaration of being in such a spot on such a day. Besides, I had studied Wainwright's description of this route and fancied that I could make out the course it took up the crag. It really did look attractive and so, forsaking the excellent path I could have followed alongside Greenup Gill, I set off through the bluebells for the crags that towered above me.

To begin with, the climb was very steep, but there was a path of sorts. Then I lost it and had to scramble on upwards, hoping that I would rejoin it in due course. The inclines grew steeper, the drops increasingly sheer. By now it was impossible to go back: there was no path and simply looking down towards the valley was enough to induce vertigo. I had to go on, but it was by no means obvious what route I should take. For a moment I was not far from losing my nerve completely and freezing to the spot. Then, quite by chance, I came upon a well-trodden path which, while not entirely to my liking for it zigzagged alarmingly above the sheer drops of Heron Crag, ultimately led me out of the danger zone and up onto the summit. The feeling of relief was overwhelming. I resolved then and there that in future, whenever a choice of routes was available to me on unfamiliar fells, I would always take the easy option.

After such a dramatic start, the rest of the day was straightforward. Sergeant's Crag, which from the valley had looked so daunting, was an easy walk from Eagle Crag. Then came a long, pathless, uphill slog over rough grass to High Raise, which offered splendid views south to the Coniston group and west to Scafell Pike and its neighbours. Closer to hand, Sergeant Man and Thunacar Knott looked so accessible that, on the spur of the moment, I added them to my route. I was even tempted to throw in some of the Langdale Pikes as well, for they were clearly visible, but fortunately I resisted the temptation, for all these additional fells were taking me ever further from my pre-planned route.

I turned about and made my way back over High Raise and on to Ullscarf. On this section of the route in particular, I was acutely aware of what a blessing it was that the weather had been dry for so long, for it meant that most of the time I could walk straight over the peat-bogs without any need for often laborious detours. There was a pleasantly cool breeze, the visibility was excellent and the bracken, which had only recently sprouted, was easy to walk through, all of which made me realize as never before that, if the weather is right, then May really is an excellent month for fell-walking.

Even so, my legs were by now seriously tired and the descent from Ullscarf to Watendlath Tarn seemed never-ending. This too was a departure from my pre-planned route, but I was beguiled by the view ahead, with three lakes - Watendlath Tarn, Derwentwater and Bassenthwaite Lake - stretching away from me one behind the other, and a good, clear path to follow. Alas, the path disappeared abruptly at Low Saddle, leaving me to zigzag about over quite rough terrain as I tried to find a reasonable way down to Watendlath. By the time I reached the tarn I was whacked, and when it came to the short climb I must make before the final descent to Rosthwaite it was almost more than I could manage. And little wonder. It turned out that I had been on the fells for eight hours, had walked fifteen miles and climbed almost three and a half thousand feet (1,065 metres). Tomorrow, I decided, would have to be a gentle day.

It was. I settled for climbing Clough Head, on the northern tip of the range which runs due south and eventually leads to Helvellyn. The climb from the Old Coach Road to White Pike is on grass but is very steep and was quite enough for my legs, still tired from yesterday. After White Pike the gradient eases, but by the time I reached the summit of Clough Head I had had more than enough climbing. Though I continued to Calfhow Pike, I was not remotely tempted to add any of the nearby Dodds, electing instead to return to the Coach Road by way of Mosedale Beck. After all, Clough Head was my fiftieth fell and I was more than happy to call it a day at that.

Next came a day of perfect weather in the far eastern fells, during which I was breaking new ground all the way. Starting from Mardale Head, I took the path up to Nan Bield Pass, skirting Small Water, a haven of tranquillity with its crystalline waters tumbling down to Haweswater far below. From the top of the pass there were fine views east and west, but they were surpassed by what the summit of Harter Fell had to offer, with its magnificent vista east along almost the entire length of Haweswater, then on to the distant Pennines.

From Harter Fell a good path on grass led me over Kentmere Pike and on to Goat Scar, where I sat in the sunshine, enjoying the view down the aptly named Longsleddale as it stretched far away into the distance. In the opposite direction I had a bird's-eye view of the Gatescarth Pass, which in April had cost me so much effort. Then I was on the move again, with another good path taking me over my final objective for the day, Shipman Knotts, by which point I had climbed one quarter of the Wainwrights or as near as dash it. By the time I had dropped down to the Kentmere valley and then made my way back over the Nan Bield Pass to my starting-point I felt, if not shattered, then certainly very tired. The question was, how much longer could I keep going without a break if the weather continued dry day after day?

The matter was resolved by my next outing, which took me to Patterdale, from where I climbed Place Fell in good style. The day was overcast, so the outstanding view of the Helvellyn range which Place Fell offers in good conditions was not available. Still, I enjoyed the long descent to Sandwick, with a cuckoo calling in the distance. My next target was Hallin Fell, a modest climb which I managed in anything but good style, my thigh muscles protesting vehemently at this second climb in one day and demanding that I stop every hundred metres or so. I placated them by taking lunch on the summit, which even on a less than perfect day offered excellent views over Ullswater. Then it was back down to the road and on to my final objective, Beda Fell. I knew that getting up this one would be a struggle and so it proved. It is a modest fell, just sixteen hundred and seventy feet (509 metres) high and offering no particular problems in ascent or descent. It was not the fell that was the problem but my legs, which had almost no climbing left in them. I had to dig really deep in order to reach the top and it was obvious that I was operating near the limits of my physical resources. Whether I liked it or not, tomorrow would have to be a rest day.

As luck would have it, the weather chose the day after my rest day to break and broke with a vengeance. It poured all night and most of the following day and threw in a strong wind to make it all the more unpleasant. Nevertheless I ventured out and managed to climb Castle Crag near Derwentwater in a downpour. It is, as Wainwright points out, "the only fell below 1,000 feet … that is awarded the 'full treatment'," i.e. a chapter to itself in his Pictorial Guide. He gives the height as approximately 985 feet, but the Ordnance Survey map gives it as 290 metres, which is 950 feet. Whatever its precise height, it fully deserves its exceptional treatment, for it is an exceptional place and has arguably the finest view over Derwentwater and the Skiddaw massif to be found in the district. Needless to say, there was no view to be had on this occasion and no incentive to linger on the summit. I was quite concerned about how the steep descent over wet slate would work out, but to my surprise it posed no problem, though crossing the River Derwent did. The stepping-stones which I had planned to use were submerged, so I continued south to the bridge at Longthwaite.

Doing the Wainwrights

I still had it in mind to tackle Great Crag, but with the rain unremitting I eventually decided to head back to Grange.

After drying out in the car and waiting for the rain to stop, I set off once more and climbed Grange Fell, an old favourite and a lovely place to explore at leisure, but not today. By the time I reached the summit the rain was lashing down again and I was soaked to the skin. Undeterred, I carried on in the direction of Great Crag, but now, after all that dry weather, the bogs were boggy, the paths had become streams, the rocks were greasy and the views non-existent. In short, I was not enjoying myself. I decided that Great Crag would have to wait for another day and retreated to dry out.

The weather remained unsettled on my final day and once again I set myself very modest targets, climbing Gowbarrow Fell above Ullswater in the rain and Little Mell Fell in unexpected sunshine, with skylarks serenading me all the way to the top. So in the end my stay finished on a high note. I had added twenty-five fells to my total, which now stood at sixty, putting me a whole month ahead of schedule after just two months. It was time to go home and give my legs the long rest they craved.

Chapter Six

June

I RETURNED to the Lake District in the middle of June for another stay of nine days, ignoring the weather forecast which held out the prospect of little but rain. Initially my luck held, for despite a decidedly damp start to my first day I was able to enjoy a late afternoon walk from Keswick to the top of Walla Crag and back in perfect conditions. After the earlier rain, the visibility was exceptionally good and the views north over Keswick to the Skiddaw massif and west over Derwentwater to Catbells and the Derwent Fells were outstanding. But after that little outing my amazing luck with the weather deserted me. Rain and more particularly low cloud became the order of the day and this view-seeking fell-walker found himself restricted, on day two, to a brief excursion up Latrigg, from where virtually nothing but thick mist verging on rain was visible, and so back to Keswick. Day three brought more of the same, except that the clouds were slightly higher, and with my trusty umbrella up most of the way I managed five simple, grassy fells to the south of Ullswater and returned damp but not soaked.

I should perhaps explain at this point that it has long been a habit of mine to take an umbrella with me whenever I am out on the fells. Years ago I made use of a rather smart city gent's-type rigid umbrella with a splendid wooden handle. Clearly visible as it protruded from the top of my rucksack, it would prompt raised eyebrows if not downright mirth in my fellow-walkers, and sometimes acute embarrassment if they were in my company when I proceeded to make use of it. I didn't care. It kept the upper half of me pretty well dry and certainly far drier than my companions in their so-called waterproof clothing, and so I took it everywhere, up to and including the summit of Ben Nevis. Later, I moved on to a collapsible version, which was certainly more discreet and easier to pack, and which was worth its weight in gold in the kind of weather I was now encountering.

It was not actually raining first thing on day four, so I decided to take a chance and tackle two modest fells with which I was unfamiliar, namely Ard Crags and Knott Rigg, above the Keskadale valley. I set off briskly from near Stair, wanting to capitalise on the conditions, which initially were pleasant but soon turned to rain. The further I progressed the less certain I became of my surroundings till, checking the map, I found that in my haste to get started I had gone up the wrong valley and was on the point of climbing not Ard Crags but Causey Pike. This was not the most auspicious of starts but fortunately I found a path which took me round the base of Ellas Crag and so to the valley I was after.

As I climbed up the steepening slope of Aikin Knott towards Ard Crags so the rain intensified and the path became more slippery. Naturally I had my umbrella up, but I was being increasingly buffeted by the wind the higher I climbed. Peering ahead through the rain, I saw a figure striding down the path towards me - the only person I would encounter on the entire walk. Just as we were on the point of passing each other, my feet slipped from under me and I toppled sideways onto my umbrella, bending some of the spokes in the process. As my fellow walker observed with a sympathetic smile, such embarrassing moments always occur just when there is someone around to witness them.

As well as being embarrassing, my tumble into the heather had accelerated the process by which the now driving rain was soaking me literally to the skin. There seemed little point in persevering with the umbrella, so I packed it away and struggled on over the summit of Ard Crags to Knott Rigg and down to Newlands Hause. As I squelched my way back along the Buttermere road, I tried to imagine what my two fells would have looked like in sunshine and, more particularly, what views I might have captured with my camera. One of these days I shall have to go back to find out.

Over the next two days I managed only Great Mell Fell and Great Crag, neither of them great in any sense despite their names, but the weather was against me and all I could do was pick off these odd-man-out fells. In point of fact, I might as well have climbed Great Crag back in May, while I was soaked to the skin after climbing Grange Fell, for the rain poured down on me again this time and left me drenched.

By now I was starting to get a bit anxious about my progress or lack of it. In six days I had climbed just eleven fells. I tried to galvanize myself into tackling more ambitious routes but it was no good. I knew I could not enjoy wandering over a succession of fell-tops in thick cloud or heavy rain, so I decided to keep chipping away at such low-level fells as I could reach given the weather.

I duly drove to Loweswater next day with the idea of climbing three unfamiliar but relatively modest fells, all of them well below two thousand feet (600 metres) and offering a good ridge route to the west of the lake. I arrived to find the cloud down to five hundred feet (150 metres). Time for plan B, not that I had one.

Luckily, the cloud was not quite so low to the east of Loweswater, so I parked near Thackthwaite and took Wainwright's direct route up Fellbarrow, which was just about clear of cloud most of the time. It was an uninspiring climb which involved picking my way, not all that successfully it must be said, over swampy ground in the lower reaches, before making a steep but dull ascent over grassland to the summit. From there the walk steadily improved as I made my way to

Low Fell, whose switchback top from Watching Crag onwards is full of interest. On a good day Low Fell, for all its modest elevation, must offer excellent views, for it occupies a commanding position between Loweswater to the west and the Vale of Lorton to the east. On this occasion I could see next to nothing of the surrounding fells, but I was afforded tantalising glimpses, between swathes of cloud, of Crummock Water, Buttermere and Loweswater, and came away feeling that I had salvaged something positive from a potentially disappointing day.

With more low cloud on day eight, I started off by tackling another modest fell, High Rigg north of Thirlmere. I made the short, steep climb from the church at the north end of the fell, whereafter the route undulated pleasantly all the way to the southern end, before dropping steeply to St John's Beck. Even on a day as overcast as this, the view over St John's in the Vale was lovely, and there were plenty of people on High Rigg to enjoy it - more than I had seen all week, in fact, but then it was a Saturday. Raven Crag was my next objective, but a sign beside the path informed me that, owing to the presence of nesting peregrine falcons, there was a close season on climbing and scrambling there until mid-July. I took this to refer to the rock-face and, as the footpath itself was still open, followed it to the summit and touched the cairn furtively, before beating a hasty retreat.

By now the visibility was quite good, so I decided to see if I could find Armboth Fell. I came out of the forestry plantation onto the moors and peered around - no sign of it! All I could do was strike out in a westerly direction across a pathless expanse of heather and marsh till I reached the only fence in the area, at which point I could follow it south and eventually find out where I was. Sure enough, I came in due course to a summit of sorts, which turned out to be High Tove.

With the bonus of an unexpected fell under my belt and knowing now just where I was, I set about walking to Armboth

Fell. This is not as simple as it sounds. Wainwright advises against making a beeline for it from High Tove because of bog between the two. Instead, he suggests heading south and then east, which is what I did. This involved a much longer and harder trek than I had anticipated, for no path east materialised and I found myself once again blazing a trail across heather and marsh and a whole series of undulations before eventually reaching the summit. Then I had to find the path down to the road beside Thirlmere, which proved no easy task. By the time I had tarmac under my feet, I was keenly aware that Armboth Fell had cost me as much effort as any fell yet, and I still had a long haul back to the car.

On my final day, with plenty of low cloud still in evidence I took a familiar route out of Grasmere, aiming to climb four modest fells. The first, Steel Fell, had its head in the clouds as I set off, but by the time I reached the summit the cloud had lifted enough for me to see more than half-way to my next objective, Calf Crag. To my delight, I reached the latter with dry feet, no mean achievement given that the route between Steel Fell and Calf Crag is notoriously boggy. The fine views which are normally to be had from Calf Crag were denied me by a murky sky which entirely concealed the distant fells, though my immediate objectives, Gibson Knott and Helm Crag, were clear enough. Helm Crag is an old favourite and I took the chance to scramble over some of the more accessible boulders and outcrops of rock on the summit and to enjoy the bird's eye-view of Grasmere. Then it was down to the car and back home, with a total haul of just twenty-one fells in nine days. Clearly, if I was to tackle the Wainwrights successfully I needed the weather on my side. I just hoped that July would serve me better than so-called flaming June had done.

Chapter Seven

July

JULY DID indeed turn up trumps. The sun blazed down from a cloudless sky as I opened my latest campaign in Coniston. The plan was an ambitious one. I wanted to try and climb all seven major fells in the vicinity of Coniston in one day rather than the two I had originally felt would be necessary.

I got a good early start and set off for Wetherlam, taking the route by Red Dell Beck. Wainwright speaks of the gradients being easy, which they certainly were, at least until I came to climb out of the valley and up to the summit, at which point the route became extremely steep, the path disappeared and the sun beat down. In no time at all I was struggling and having to stop every twenty metres or so to regain my breath. As these enforced pauses became longer and more frequent, doubts began to creep into my mind. Was this ascent more than I could cope with? Was I paying the price for the fact that I had not gone to the gym once in the last three weeks? Should I stop and have a proper rest or even turn back? If I had felt the slightest hint of chest pain I would, I am sure, have abandoned the walk, but fortunately I experienced no such thing and at length emerged onto the summit of Wetherlam. The moment of doubt was over and the rest of the day was sheer joy. Later on, when I was able to look back from Coniston Old Man at the route I had taken, I was not surprised that I had had moments of doubt, for the final section up Wetherlam is a very steep climb indeed.

Invigorated by the marvellous views in every direction, including no less than five lakes as well as Morecambe Bay, I headed for Swirl How, which involved another steep but thankfully short climb. Then came a pleasant stroll over to Great Carrs, with swifts whizzing past me at ankle-level and sometimes, more alarmingly, at head-height. From Great Carrs it was a simple climb up to Grey Friar, passing en route the spot where, in October 1944, a Halifax bomber had crashed into the hillside. That brought with it sombre thoughts of yesterday's bus and tube bombings in London, which formed a strange and terrible contrast with the beauty of the day and the surroundings. I went on my way, feeling more acutely conscious than ever of how lucky I was to be in such a place on such a day.

I stopped for lunch on the summit of Grey Friar, from where there were excellent views north over the Wrynose Pass and the fells beyond, and south to my three remaining targets for the day, Dow Crag, Brim Fell and Coniston Old Man. After lunch, I made my way to Dow Crag, where I gingerly touched the topmost rock then hastily withdrew, for the summit is perched at the very top of crags which fall away precipitously, making it a perfect spot for inducing vertigo. Next came the final steep climb of the day, from Goat's Hause up to Brim Fell. It was all I could do to drag my protesting legs up this one, and I knew then that I had no more climbing in me. Fortunately, the way to Coniston Old Man from Brim Fell is by the gentlest of inclines and soon I was on the summit, taking in yet another superb panoramic view.

To descend to Coniston I took the route through the old mine workings. Wainwright is unusually disparaging about this route, but I didn't care. It was the most direct way back to the car and that was all that mattered. Even so, it felt very long, very steep and very stony. Later I discovered that the total ascent had been four thousand three hundred and twenty-five feet (1,320 metres), which was the most I had ever managed in a single day.

Doing the Wainwrights

It had been a long day too, for I had been out on the fells for seven and a half hours. No wonder I felt so weary. What had made this outing not only possible but outstanding was the weather, which had been perfect throughout, witness the twenty or more photographs I had taken. What a difference from June!

After that, an easy day was in order and I tackled three undemanding fells, Lank Rigg, Crag Fell and Grike, which lie to the south of Ennerdale Water. It was another beautiful day, which was just as well, for trying to find the way on and off Lank Rigg in poor visibility would be a nightmare - it is all rounded, grassy slopes with precious few features. It is also quite remote. Lose your way here and you could have a real problem. On this occasion, however, I was serenaded by skylarks as I ate my lunch on the summit, while enjoying the views out to the Isle of Man and the Mull of Galloway. I also enjoyed the telescoping of time to be achieved by lining up the prehistoric tumulus near the summit of Lank Rigg with the distant but clearly visible site of the nuclear reprocessing plant at Seascale. It was Wainwright who had alerted me to this juxtaposition of two reference points, which between them embraced just about the whole of human history in this area.

After lunch, I headed for Crag Fell, enjoying the chance to stride out on grass, as I made my way up to and over Whoap, and then across moorland. The path up to the summit of Crag Fell was clear and a pleasure to climb: steep but not too steep, with steadily improving views across open countryside and the enticing prospect of what lay just beyond the crest ahead. I reached the top and was elated to find myself on a wonderful vantage-point offering splendid views north over Ennerdale Water to the Solway Firth and east along the lake to Steeple, Pillar and the Buttermere Fells. After more camera work, a brisk walk took me to the top of Grike and I had my three fells for the day without undue effort. A forestry track led me back to the road and the car, where one further spectacle awaited me. As

I was removing my boots, a pack of hounds came charging across the countryside, working hard in the heat by the sound of it. They crossed the road not far from where I was parked - there were men on hand with flags to stop the traffic - and disappeared into the distance. I had seen my first ever hound trail.

Next day it was back to serious business as I set about tackling Scafell Pike and co. The weather remained good and, if anything, was even hotter than the previous two days. Despite an early start from Seathwaite, I was lathered by the time I reached Styhead Tarn. It felt as though I had already done one major climb, whereas of course I was still no more than half-way towards the Scafell group.

I took the corridor route as far as the Lingmell col, and just before reaching the latter came upon some strange, elongated rings or horseshoe shapes in a group of rocks. I counted eleven of them and thought they looked a bit like fossilized oysters. At the col I turned north and climbed to the summit of Lingmell, my first fell of the day, by which time I had been climbing more or less all the way for two and a quarter hours. I absorbed the dramatic view north across the valley separating Lingmell from Great Gable and which makes the latter look so awesome, then retraced my steps to the col. From here there was a scarcely less dramatic view of Scafell Crag, which fortunately did not form part of my itinerary for the day. After a much-needed pause for refreshment, I set about climbing once more, this time up the well-worn track to the summit of Scafell Pike.

As normal, there was quite a crowd on the top. I had almost joined them when an RAF rescue helicopter appeared and hovered overhead. Inside the open doorway a member of the crew was waving down at us. I half expected someone to be winched off the top but, after circling a couple of times, the helicopter headed off for other parts. I presume they were just checking that all was well. It is certainly nice to know that they are there if needed.

With cloud blowing in from the south, I stopped just long enough to take in the full extent of the views to the north, with Derwentwater, the Skiddaw massif and Blencathra all clearly visible though more than thirteen miles distant. Then I was on the move again, making the steep descent towards Broad Crag. This turned out to be a lot steeper than I remembered and quite badly eroded, and I found myself thinking that if I could manage that, which I could, then surely I could manage just about anything. I made a detour to visit the summit of Great End, another excellent viewpoint offering a dramatic close-up of Broad Crag and the uppermost part of Scafell Pike as well as long views over Lingmell right out to the Isle of Man. After that I made for Styhead Tarn, but turned off the path at Sprinkling Tarn in order to try and find the summit of Seathwaite Fell, my fourth and final target for the day.

As Wainwright makes clear, this is no easy task, for there is a profusion of rocky outcrops which could lay claim to being the highest point, while what is generally regarded as the summit is clearly not. The only solution was to try and visit all the likely candidates, including the putative summit with its cairn, but this required a lot more effort than I had bargained for towards the end of an already tiring day. It had been a similar story in April on Rosthwaite Fell. It is as if these lesser fells are determined to compensate for their lack of altitude by making life as difficult as possible for those who would stand on their summit.

Eventually, having satisfied myself that I had visited all the likely contenders for the highest point, I had to think about how I would get off the fell. One option was to rejoin the Styhead Tarn path where I had left it but, now that I was at the north end of the fell and wanting to head further north still, I was reluctant to start by heading south. I consulted Wainwright, who suggests a couple of ways off down the north-west side of the fell to Styhead Gill and I decided to attempt something similar. Steering well clear of Aaron Crags, I came down a very steep and pathless slope without difficulty and joined the good track back to Seathwaite.

It was again very hot on this final section of the route and I found myself fantasising about iced lollies long before I treated myself to one on reaching the farm. By then I had been out for seven hours and, after all the rocks and boulders I had been walking over the entire day, the tarmac felt blissful to my feet. I fell into the car exhausted but happy. It had been another excellent day and Seathwaite Fell was a bonus, for I had not really thought that I would manage it this time. I now had ninety-five fells behind me, including the first and highest of the fells over three thousand feet. As for tomorrow, the only plan that would come into my head was... Rest Day!

My resolve to take it easy lasted till tea-time next day, at which point feelings of guilt prompted by the glorious weather got the better of me and I did a simple walk out of Keswick, climbing Bleaberry Fell and High Seat. The path up Bleaberry Fell had been massively upgraded since I was last there and the sun had largely dried out the boggy ground between that fell and High Seat, so that I managed the entire out-and-back trip without once getting my feet wet, something I would never have thought possible on that route. Both fell-tops offered panoramic views which were particularly good in the early evening light. As I made my way back to Keswick, paragliders circled lazily in the sky, their silent motion emphasizing the perfect tranquillity of the scene I had been privileged to enjoy.

I was now poised to take my tally of fells past the one hundred mark, for I had it in mind to finish off this July visit in style by climbing the Helvellyn group. When the day dawned hotter than ever, with talk of the temperature reaching 27 celsius, I changed my mind and decided to settle for doing just two of the fells in the group, Catstycam and Birkhouse Moor. I am glad I did. As I set off from Patterdale, it was already very warm and there was the lovely smell of hay-making in the air. The approach to Catstycam, following the course of Glenridding Beck, was a delight, all gentle gradients and patches of cool shade. But then the path steepened as it climbed towards Red Tarn and, with no shade to be had, I was really feeling the heat by the time I had the summit in my sights.

Wainwright describes the climb up the east shoulder as "easy, on grass all the way." I must say that is not how I would describe it. Quite apart from the fact that these days the grass has given way to a river of stones, it proved a steep and increasingly exposed climb as the shoulder narrowed and the slopes fell away ever more sharply on both sides. The summit itself is extremely pointy and one glance down the far side made me thankful that I had not attempted the north-west ridge.

I was half expecting the path off the summit in the direction of Swirral Edge to be equally fearsome, but it proved to be quite gentle. Indeed I felt so comfortable with it that I stopped half-way down for lunch and sat watching the tiny figures tackling Swirral Edge - most definitely not for me! - and Striding Edge, which I have climbed in the past but whose final section now looked much too fierce for me to stomach. After lunch I dropped down to Red Tarn and sat for a while with my feet in the water - nice and refreshing for me but less good for the environment! Then came a simple walk over Birkhouse Moor, followed by a very long descent, much of it on a rock staircase, to Glenridding. By then I had done about as much as I could manage. I treated myself to a bottle of chilled chocolate milk, a rare departure from my normal low fat diet but which in the circumstances was sheer bliss, then set off for home with a tantalizing ninety-nine fells under my belt.

On returning to the Lakes at the end of July, I had grandiose plans for tackling many of the highest and most remote fells, but the weather put paid to all that. On my first day, the cloud base remained obstinately at around fifteen hundred feet (450 metres), so I settled for climbing Sheffield Pike and Glenridding Dodd, hardly the highest or remotest of fells but at least manageable in those conditions. Besides, neither of them really fitted in with any other route, so I would have to do them separately sooner or later.

Comforting myself with these thoughts, I set off from Dockray, wearing scarcely less than I normally wear in mid-winter. By the time I reached Glencoyne Head I was into the mist, which thickened steadily as I climbed to the summit of Sheffield Pike, my one hundredth fell. Not quite the auspicious moment I had envisaged, with panoramic views from some towering peak, but never mind. A hundred fells are a hundred fells, no matter what the view or lack of it.

The plan now was to continue over Heron Pike and drop down to Glenridding Dodd, but I had only to look around me to know that I would never manage that. Trying to find my way in the blanket of cloud that surrounded me was quite beyond my strictly limited powers of navigation, especially on a route which was not simple and where crags abounded. I turned tail and made my way back to the Glencoyne path, which I followed down to the edge of Glencoyne Wood.

Now I was out of the mist and could at least see where I was going. All I had to do was follow a wall which passes below Heron Pike till it meets another wall at right-angles and then follow that one onto Glenridding Dodd. It sounds simple enough and in a purely navigational sense it is. But it should be said that the path I was following was little more than a sheep-trod through waist-high bracken so thick that I could only tell by feel what was under my feet, which did not exactly make for rapid progress. In addition, though it was not actually raining there was enough moisture in the air and more particularly on the bracken to leave me soaked to the skin from the waist down, just as if I had waded out into the sea.

Doing the Wainwrights

Eventually I made it to the point where the two walls met. Now I was out of the bracken and could revel in the profound stillness. No traffic, no voices, absolute silence. This was something very special, yet when it was finally disturbed the effect was quite wonderful, for what I heard was the distant pealing of church bells coming, so far as I could judge, from Glenridding far below me.

As the top of Glenridding Dodd was well below the level of the cloud, I explored many of the hummocks to be found there, all of them clothed now in purple heather, and enjoyed the views over Ullswater which, even on a day as overcast as this, were stunning. Then it was a case of finding a way down.

Two solutions offered themselves. One was a very steep path down to Glenridding, but as my destination was Dockray I ruled that out. The other was to retrace my steps as far as the Glencoyne path, but I could not face all that wet bracken again. It was time to try my luck, so I followed a path which was dropping down towards Ullswater and hoped for the best. It started well and soon I was following the course of Mossdale Beck, which for my purposes was ideal. However, the path became progressively less distinct as I advanced and eventually I was reduced to ploughing my way through walls of bracken far taller than I was, before finally emerging onto the road beside Ullswater.

At this point my problems should have been over, but following the road as it hugs the shores of Ullswater is not a comfortable experience, particularly with all the traffic that a Saturday in late July can generate. When a footpath across Glencoyne Park offered itself, I gladly took it, only to find that it was leading me directly towards a large herd of cattle, including a good many calves and, for all I knew, a bull as well. I diplomatically adjusted my direction by ninety degrees, doubled my speed and was glad when I was back on the road, for in my view that was definitely the lesser of two evils. By the time I reached Dockray I had been out for five and a half hours and what should have been a relatively easy day did not feel that way at all. Still, I had now passed the one hundred mark and the half-way point beckoned.

Next day saw me at Seathwaite, with Esk Pike, Bowfell, Crinkle Crags (possibly) and Rossett Pike in my sights. It was surprisingly quiet as I climbed up the usually popular path by Grains Gill, though there was a party of three - two men and a young lad - just ahead of me. The lad was lagging some way behind and, when I caught him up, he informed me that they were heading for Scafell Pike. Evidently a degree of bribery was involved for, shortly afterwards, I heard him yell out, in a voice that carried for miles: "I want my sausage roll!" I hope he did not have to wait till the summit of Scafell Pike before he got it.

At Esk Hause the cloud was blowing in intermittently, but I was able to see my way up to Esk Pike well enough. However, just as I was nearing the summit and wondering about the route down the other side, the mist suddenly closed in, reducing visibility to a few metres. I do not know why it is that conditions so often deteriorate like this just when one is uncertain of one's route and most prone to discouragement, but I know that it happens time and again. On this occasion I was fortunate, for the mist soon cleared and by the time I reached Bowfell visibility was good and remained that way.

Now I had to decide whether or not to continue to Crinkle Crags, which I could see clearly. I consulted Wainwright and found that the highest Crinkle was the fourth out of five from Bowfell. I calculated that it would add the best part of two hours to my total time and that I would probably not feel much like visiting Rossett Pike afterwards, in which case I would have to make a separate excursion simply to climb that. Taking comfort from Wainwright's observation that the Crinkles are too good to do in a hurry, I settled for exploring Bowfell in leisurely fashion, and there is certainly plenty to explore.

Doing the Wainwrights

Though I had seen it before, I still found the vast surface of the Great Slab, tilting upwards at such a dramatic angle, hugely impressive, and the River of Stones that runs down one side of it is scarcely less spectacular. Indeed Bowfell surely boasts some of the finest mountain scenery to be found in the Lake District and my camera worked overtime as I attempted to capture the drama of Bowfell Buttress, with minuscule fell-walkers on the climbers' traverse far below at its foot; or the shattered rocks that litter the fell-top, leaning at crazy angles above huge drops; or the spectacular views east over the Langdale Pikes and valley or north-west towards the Scafell massif.

At length I tore myself away and proceeded to Rossett Pike, which I had not visited before. Looking down on it from Bowfell, it had seemed so tiny that it came as a surprise to find that it is over two thousand feet (600 metres) high. It certainly makes an excellent viewpoint, and I sat on the summit enjoying the view of the Langdale Pikes and the valley below and savouring the absolute stillness. All too soon it was time to head back to Seathwaite. This involved climbing up to Esk Hause first, and by the time I made it to the top I was feeling very glad that I had decided against doing the Crinkles. Now at least my route was downhill all the way and the only problem was how to get my legs into shape for the next day's activities which, I felt sure, would see me pass the half-way mark in this venture of mine. But that is another story.

Chapter Eight

On being a wimp

AUGUST THE FIRST. I am feeling decidedly nervous about my plans for the day, which involve climbing Hard Knott, Slight Side and Scafell, for this is all unknown territory, including the road with its two passes - the Wrynose and the Hardknott - about both of which I have serious misgivings. However, if I am to climb Hard Knott there appears to be no real alternative to driving to the top of the pass, so that is what I must do.

As for Hard Knott itself, it looks from Wainwright's illustrations to be daunting, with crags abounding and the only way up involving a run of scree (I do not like scree) which can be easily missed on the way back down, with potentially serious consequences. Having digested that information, I am not at all sure that I am going to make it to the top, or down again if I do. And then there is Scafell, which has always looked just about impregnable whenever I have viewed it from the vicinity of Scafell Pike. True, I have chosen what appears to be the only easy way up, but ease, like beauty, is in the eye of the beholder and I am not at all sure that what seemed easy to Wainwright will seem so to me. Still, I cannot keep putting these fells off forever, so with considerable trepidation I head south.

The approach road from Little Langdale is something of a trial in itself, all narrow twists and turns with stone walls on either side making progress an act of faith. I drive along at a snail's pace, ready to do an emergency stop at any moment and feeling about as relaxed as a sky-diver whose parachute has failed to open.

Then comes the Wrynose Pass. It too is narrow and twisty, with some fierce gradients thrown in for good measure. Somehow I negotiate it, if not comfortably then at least without any moments of crisis. Thanking my lucky stars that I made an early start and so have encountered no oncoming traffic as yet, I turn onto the Hardknott Pass.

Here the gradients are so steep and the bends so acute that it is all I can do to maintain forward momentum. I am subliminally conscious of passing through glorious countryside but I cannot take my eyes off the road - or the car bonnet whenever the road disappears from sight - for a second. Then comes a moment of sheer panic when I realize that, although I am in second gear, I am not going to make it to the top. I slap on the hand-brake, hoping and praying that it will hold the car on a gradient so steep that, if I start rolling back, I will be off the road and into the boulders in a matter of seconds. Trying not to think about what happens if a car comes the other way - I am slewed across the road on a hairpin bend - I do a hill-start the like of which I have never done before and crawl to the top in first.

I am supposed to be looking for a cairn which marks the top of the pass, but I fail to spot it and only realize I am at the top when almost immediately the road starts dropping no less steeply than it had climbed. For one awful moment I believe that I have missed my chance and will have to drive all the way down to the bottom, turn round and drive back up again. Then, just before the descent starts in earnest, I spot a pull-in big enough for just one car, and what is more it is empty. I seize the opportunity, park the car and switch off the ignition, but instead of leaping into action I just sit there for several minutes, feeling quite wrung out. And that's before I've even walked a step!

Eventually I pull on my boots, get out of the car and take stock of the situation. I find little cause for comfort. As a rule,

On being a wimp

I try to ensure that I have about ten minutes of easy walking before I tackle anything steep, in order to give my body a chance to get warmed up and so avoid putting my heart under undue strain. But there is no scope here for warming up of any sort, since there is no flat ground to be seen in any direction. All I can do is start on the climb up Hard Knott, taking it as gently as possible while at the same time trying to psych myself up for the apparently inescapable scree-run that lies in wait for me. Normally speaking, I will do anything to avoid loose scree, so when I find that the path has changed since Wainwright's day and now follows a grassy course, I am delighted. Moreover, a new fence has been erected, marking the position of the path perfectly clearly, so there is now no question of my being unable to find it on the way back down. With my fears allayed, I proceed to the summit.

The climb turns out to be a perfectly simple one and it takes me just thirty minutes to reach the top of Hard Knott. Even so, my mouth is dry and my legs are struggling, a consequence of the adrenalin rush while tackling the Hardknott Pass, no doubt. The summit is deserted, desolate even, as is the entire scene spread out before me. A thick blanket of grey cloud obscures the upper reaches of the fells ahead, and what bit is visible looks dark and forbidding. I try to think positively, focussing on my next targets, Slight Side and Scafell. But as I peer across to what I take to be Scafell, it looks utterly daunting, so there is not much encouragement to be taken from that.

I make my way back to the car, preparing myself mentally for the drive down to Eskdale. It turns out to be not nearly as traumatic as the drive up, but as I park beside the River Esk I know one thing for certain. Nothing will ever induce me to drive over the Hardknott Pass again.

I set off on my second walk at 10.45 and have barely started to climb out of the valley when an RAF jet suddenly screams over Hardknott Pass and thunders immediately overhead.

Somehow that seems symptomatic of a day on which relaxation is simply not possible. I find the climb up to Slight Side a struggle, even though the gradients are generally easy. I know that my legs are tired from the previous two days, but I also know that I am not on form today and as a result I feel more than usually apprehensive. With not a soul in sight for mile after mile, I have repeatedly to do battle with the "What if ...?" syndrome. What if I start feeling unwell out here in the middle of nowhere? What if there is no signal on my mobile phone? (There almost certainly isn't). No matter what I try, I cannot completely dispel my anxiety.

When finally I reach the top of Slight Side, the summit cairn provides a further and unexpected challenge, for it is perched on top of exposed, bare rock. Somehow or other I clamber up to a point from which I can just about touch it and then I start wondering about the wisdom of going on to Scafell. There is still a lot of cloud ahead and every now and then it briefly exposes a fearsome-looking pike surrounded by near vertical scree-slopes. How on earth am I going to get up there? I have almost convinced myself that, in the circumstances, the sensible course of action is to retrace my steps when, suddenly, the cloud lifts completely and I find that what I had taken for Scafell is in fact a pinnacle of rock forming part of Scafell Pike. Scafell itself is further to the west and, now that I can see the path leading almost to the top, I appreciate that it is perfectly straightforward. I set off in much better heart.

The route indeed proves unproblematic and on the summit I meet the first people I have seen since leaving Eskdale. The views, whenever the cloud lifts, are quite wonderful, particularly over Wast Water, while away to the east Scafell Pike is clearly as popular as ever. It is a source of considerable satisfaction to realize that, though I had not planned it this way, this great fell marks the half-way point in my endeavours. I permit myself to enjoy the views for a few minutes, but do not explore and so see

Route 3. Spring lambs and the northern face of Mellbreak, which I chickened out of.

Route 5. The bridge at Sadgill, last stop before the long, long haul up the Gatescarth Pass.

Route 6. The summit of Allen Crags, looking towards
Great End. Only the tiny patches of snow betray
the fact that it's April.

Route 8. I've barely started and just look at the view!
The head of Ullswater from Arnison Crag.

Our cat Teazel "helping" with the planning process.

Route 9. Crag Fell seen across Ennerdale Water at the start of the most perfect day in May.

Route 9. The abandoned boot on Scoat Fell,
with Red Pike beyond.

Route 9. Scoat Fell and Steeple (the bump on the right)
seen from Pillar.

Route 11. The south-east face of Eagle Crag.
Not recommended for those who suffer from vertigo!

Route 13. Haweswater and the Pennines seen from
Harter Fell in more glorious May weather.

Route 17. The Skiddaw massif from the summit
of Walla Crag during a break in the June rain.

Route 21. No doubt about the prevailing wind up here!
The slopes of Great Mell Fell, with Gowbarrow Fell beyond.

Route 23. A tantalising glimpse of the view south
from Low Fell. It just about sums up the
weather conditions in June.

Route 26. Real summer weather at last.
The Coniston fells and Youth Hostel in July.

Route 26. The summit of Dow Crag, a perfect place
for inducing vertigo.

Route 28. "On top of the world!" The view north from the
summit of Scafell Pike, with Great Gable (right) and Kirk
Fell (left) in the foreground.

Route 28. A fine view from a little fell: north-east towards
Borrowdale and Derwentwater from Seathwaite Fell.

Route 30. Catstycam from Glenridding Beck.
The north-west ridge appears unremittingly steep.
I tackled this one from the east.

Route 32. The Great Slab and the River of Stones on Bowfell, surely one of the most dramatic sights in the Lake District.

Route 32. Beauty savoured in tranquillity:
the Langdale valley from Rossett Pike.

Route 33b. The high point of a daunting day:
looking west over Wast Water from the summit of Scafell.

Route 34. Hopegill Head from Grisedale Pike.

Route 35a. The trig point and, behind it, the true summit (which defeated me) of Harter Fell. The walker in red gives scale to that slab of rock.

Route 35b. Wast Water and Yewbarrow from Whin Rigg. Fortunately, the wind was blowing me away from the cliff edge.

Route 36. North over Bassenthwaite from the summit of
Dodd - a vast improvement since Wainwright's day!

Route 37. Crummock Water and Grasmoor from Red Pike.

Route 38. The Caldew valley in all its summer glory,
with Carrock Fell beyond.

Route 39. Easedale Tarn from the foot of Tarn Crag,
during a fruitless search for "the path".

Route 40. On course for the World Masters' Fell-running Championships over Lonscale Fell and Skiddaw.

Competitors in the World Masters
Fell-Running Championship.

Route 42a. Great Door, on the south ridge of Yewbarrow.
Thank heavens for the path on the right!

Route 42a. All flags flying on the summit of Yewbarrow.
Beyond is Great Gable.

nothing of Mickledore and the huge crags to be found there. The truth of the matter is that, now I am up here, I am anxious to get off the summit and clear of the cloud, pockets of which keep blowing in from the west.

Originally I had intended to return to Eskdale by way of Burnmoor Tarn, so making a round of it, but I now decide that, rather than trying to find an unfamiliar path, I will return by my outward route, which is also the most direct. I have barely left the summit before the sun comes out fully and, for the first time today, I relax properly, secure in the fact that I know where I am going and that my route is downhill all the way.

As I look down from the slopes of Scafell towards Slight Side, I am struck by the aptness of the name for that fell, whereas on my outward journey it had seemed like a taunt as I laboured endlessly up its slopes. The walk back to Eskdale is comfortable and relaxed. True, I now have to drive back to base after a long and tiring day, but at least I don't have to face those passes again. I drive right round the western and northern perimeters of the Lake District, which is a lot further than my outward journey but worth every mile. My overriding feeling is one of relief. What I had set out to do today with such trepidation is now behind me!

*****

Nobody reading this account can fail to realize what a wimp I am. How this has come about I do not know, for in my younger days I would have done the whole excursion without a second thought. Indeed I recall getting lost in a complete white-out on High Street many years ago and plunging down the nearest slope in thick snow with nothing more on my feet than a pair of wellies. Foolish yes, wimpish no.

Age, it seems, has changed all that, aided and abetted no doubt by the experience of serious illness. For those few months when I was living with unstable angina, it became a habit to listen to my body, registering the slightest aches in case they were significant and trying to be prepared for a crisis which could and sometimes did come out of the blue. After the angioplasty, I had to build up my confidence little by little, proving to myself that I could do things by doing them, but a legacy of apprehensiveness has evidently persisted. The question is what, if anything, am I going to do about it?

There is the John Ridgway approach, which involves confronting and conquering your demons. You are afraid of heights? You will climb to the top of the ship's mast and stay there as it swings through an arc of ninety degrees or more. You don't like being underwater? You will swim right under the boat from one side to the other. I can appreciate the virtues of this approach and I suppose that, on a very modest level, I may even have practised it myself. But proving to yourself that you can still climb mountains by doing so does not really amount to confronting your demons, the essence of which, it seems to me, is an apprehension verging on terror through which you force yourself in order to come out the other side a stronger person. If such a process enables you to put that particular fear behind you, fair enough. If it doesn't and the demons are still there next time around, then in my view it is no way to live.

Another approach is simply to accept that you are a wimp and avoid all those circumstances in which wimpishness might come into play. No confronting of demons, no terror and above all no risks. But that way lies a life which, with every passing year, becomes more and more restricted, till in the end everything that is not part of a well-tried and tested routine has to be shunned. Your horizons have closed in and become bars.

My approach falls somewhere between the two and, if I am honest, is significantly nearer the second. Thus I psych myself up a bit in order to tackle fells with which I am unfamiliar and which sound as though they might test my nerve a little or even quite a lot. Steeple and Hard Knott are examples that spring to mind. In a sense, I suppose, the whole attempt to do the Wainwrights is taking me into unknown territory and testing my resolve. But having said that, there are various ways of going about it. More often than not I have the choice of whether to make life hard or easy for myself and in the overwhelming majority of cases I settle for the easy option. My experience on Eagle Crag is the exception that proves the rule, for there I chose the difficult route and paid for it. It is not an experience I would care to repeat, just as I would not choose to tackle Cofa Pike or Swirral Edge or Sharp Edge. I would rather be a happy wimp on a route I can enjoy than try to prove myself a hard man by sweating it out on a route I find terrifying.

Besides, I take comfort from the fact that in a sense we are all wimps, for there is always someone whose exploits overshadow anything we may have done. When it comes to the fells, one has only to read Richard Askwith's book Feet in the Clouds to realize the truth of this remark. It relates all sorts of mind-boggling exploits, the most directly relevant of which is Joss Naylor's record of just seven days, one hour and twenty-five minutes for all two hundred and fourteen Wainwright fells. Even if I were to climb every single fell by the hardest route possible, the fact that I am taking a year over it makes it a wimp's picnic by comparison. Joss set his record when he was fifty. Since then, Everest has been climbed by a blind man, by a fifteen-year-old girl and by a seventy-year-old man whose father could still, at ninety-nine, make the descent down the glaciated Vallée Blanche from the foot of Mont Blanc to Chamonix! In that sort of company, 99.9% of the world's population are wimps.

In effect, we all have to find that particular level of risk or challenge with which we feel able to cope and this is a life-long process, for what we can cope with, mentally as well as physically, changes with age. The truth of the old adage "Know yourself" is proved once again. It is good to test the limits occasionally, to stop the horizons closing in too much and maybe even push them back a little, but I see no point in making a fetish of it and becoming miserable in the process.

If, with age and illness, I have become more apprehensive about scrambling over rock or coping with bad weather conditions, if I am more prone to vertigo when confronted by sheer drops, then I had better face up to these things and find a way round them. So I avoid the really testing routes entirely and treat what Wainwright somewhat euphemistically calls "airy" locations with extreme circumspection. When I do tackle what I expect to be a demanding route, I keep in mind Jen's pithy advice: "If in doubt, don't." It is (nearly) always possible to change plans, to turn back. To do so may be less heroic than pressing on regardless, but it is also less nerve-racking and often more responsible. In bad weather conditions - high winds, low cloud, ice underfoot - I put enjoyment and personal safety ahead of risk-taking and opt for low-level walks. If that makes me a wimp, so be it.

On that day in April when I set out to climb Mellbreak, I could have forced myself to tackle the ascent up the north ridge and I might perhaps have made it to the top, but I am quite sure I would not have enjoyed myself and I might very well have lost my nerve half-way up. Given the way I felt about it, to persist in my initial choice of route when there were other ways of reaching the top would have been highly perverse. The objective, after all, was to reach the summit by a route, any route, and to enjoy myself in the process. And that, by and large, is what I have done throughout this exercise. With the single exception of Mellbreak, I have never had to abandon a route because it was too challenging, which says a good deal more about my care in choosing routes I feel I can cope with than about my determination. It also goes to show that, in doing the Wainwrights as in life more generally, where there's a wimp there's a way.

On being a wimp

*****

After the terrors of Hard Knott and Scafell I was in need of a more relaxed outing, so next day I drove to Braithwaite and set about climbing Grisedale Pike, Hopegill Head and Whiteside. Having walked this route more than once before, I knew I could cope with it even though the fells in question could and indeed did look daunting at times. Besides, the paths were so clear that even I could not lose them, the sun was shining and there were a fair few walkers about, so everything combined to make me feel wholly at ease.

While my legs were far from fresh, I was still able to get stuck into the long, steep climb up Grisedale Pike. Indeed, I was congratulating myself on the business-like fashion in which I was completing it, when a fell-runner and his border collie swept past me as if I were standing still and charged on up to the summit. What wouldn't I have given to have just a small part of their overflowing energy!

From the top the views were good and the way to Hopegill Head was clear and presented no problem. What was slightly problematic was the ridge route between Hopegill Head and Whiteside. There is a part of this route where the ridge narrows, falling away sharply on both sides, and where a bit of scrambling is involved. Needless to say, Wainwright regards this as "the best section of the journey", but I was glad to get it behind me, though of course it was all to do again on my way back once I had visited the summit of Whiteside. Curiously it seemed less testing on the return journey and I even entertained notions of adding one or two more fells to the day's route, but my legs had other ideas. On reaching Coledale Hause, they took the downward path to Braithwaite without any protest from my head, which merely observed that the wind was picking up and I had probably had the best of the day, though it was only about

Doing the Wainwrights

1pm! By the time I reached Braithwaite I knew that my legs had been right. I had worked really hard over these last four days, even though I had only eleven fells to show for it, and I was more than ready to head back home and rest up in preparation for the next visit.

Chapter Nine

August

ON 19 AUGUST I was back in action, this time with an ambitious double target. In an attempt to mop up the remaining fells in the far south-west of the Lake District, I wanted to climb Green Crag and Harter Fell from the Eskdale valley, then drive to the foot of Irton Pike and tackle Whin Rigg and Illgill Head, above Wast Water. All of this was unknown territory to me and I had no idea whether my plan was feasible or not.

It was so misty when I woke that, peering through the caravan window, I could not see the trees in the adjacent field, but the mist gradually burned off and by the time I set out from the Woolpack Inn in Eskdale the sun was shining. The walk up to Green Crag was a delight all the way, starting with a lovely crossing of the River Esk by way of Doctor Bridge. Once I got onto the fellside the heather was full out and the air was heavy with the scent of honey. At one point a hawk hovered not far above me for several minutes, clearly visible against the deep blue of the sky, and that was a moment to savour.

A good path took me to the top, which offered a fine view of Harter Fell, but with no direct route linking the two I had to drop back down towards Eskdale before starting to climb all over again. I compounded the effort required by missing the direct ascent, which goes up the west flank of Harter Fell, and so found myself hiking half-way round the foot of the fell before meeting a path which climbed it from the south-east. Still, the top was certainly worth the effort. It's a fascinating place with a lot of rocky outcrops and two summits - the official one, a trig-point, which I duly touched, and the true summit, an imposing outcrop of rock which I attempted to climb but failed. Having missed the direct route on the way up, I made a point of following it on the way down and so had the benefit of a round trip, reaching the car nearly five hours after setting off.

I drove immediately to the starting-point for my second walk of the day, and then deliberated. It was now after 3.30pm and my legs were tired. In addition, I had a drive of more than fifty miles back to base. Should I postpone this second walk? I toyed with the idea for a moment or two but, given that I was on the spot and the weather was fine, it seemed too good an opportunity to miss and I thought it would do no harm to stretch myself a little. So off I set for Whin Rigg.

A good forestry track led me in due course to grazing-land which had been badly churned up by cattle. Fortunately they were not in evidence and the ground was hard enough to allow me to walk over the mire rather than through it: in wet conditions this part of the route would be very trying indeed. From the top of Whin Rigg I followed the escarpment all the way to my final destination, Illgill Head. The wind on the ridge was very strong, but fortunately it was blowing me away from the sheer drops rather than towards them and I found the combination of the wind, the long views and the good going underfoot utterly exhilarating. Needless to say I did not visit either of the viewpoints illustrated by Wainwright, both of which struck me as far too exposed for comfort, but I did take numerous photographs of the startling views down to Wast Water.

Having visited both cairns on Illgill Head, I turned about and made my way back. About a quarter of a mile before the forestry plantation began, I spotted the cattle responsible for churning up the grazing-land. There were a lot of them and they were heading my way. With no alternative to the path I was on,

I put on a spurt and reached the final fence before they could come between me and the stile. What I would have done had I arrived on the scene a few minutes later to find them blocking my path I have no idea, for I was far too tired by that stage to make any sort of substantial detour. Indeed I discovered later that I had covered sixteen and a half miles and climbed four thousand nine hundred and fifty feet (1,510 metres), easily eclipsing anything I had done before in a single day. It had certainly been worth it, for I had had two excellent walks and had now climbed all the south-westerly fells between Wast Water and Coniston Water. I tumbled into bed, tired but delighted with the way the day had gone and with not a clue about what I would do come tomorrow.

I would like to be able to report that the following day dawned bright and beautiful. No doubt it did, but I had such a slow start that it was noon before I was on the move, climbing Dodd in the northern fells from the Forestry Commission car park at Mirehouse. These days Dodd is a very different place from when Wainwright visited it, at which time it was entirely covered by pine trees. Now the upper part has been clear-felled to reveal the spectacular views north, west and south, and a good path has been created to the summit, where a fine stone marks the highest spot. It was a beautiful day, with a fresh breeze to disperse any heat-haze so that the views, particularly along Bassenthwaite towards the Solway Firth and Dumfriesshire, were outstanding.

I made my way next to White Stones, then took the steep path up to Carl Side, finding the climb really tough after yesterday's exertions. As the path is sheltered by higher ground to the west and north, there was no breeze to offset the heat of the sun, which is doubtless why several million mayflies had elected to hover over the path and the beautiful carpet of purple heather on either side of it. After numerous stops, I finally made it to the top where at last I escaped the mayflies.

Doing the Wainwrights

Carl Side is an unsatisfying, almost flat summit, a great disappointment after all the effort expended in reaching it, so I did not linger but made my way to Long Side, from where I had good views over the summit of Dodd to the distant fells beyond. The ridge route over Ullock Pike was a delight, the ridge being narrow but the ground falling away obliquely on either flank so that I felt not the slightest hint of vertigo. Then came the long descent of the Edge, offering splendid views north and west whenever it was possible to take my eyes off the path, which has deteriorated quite badly and is in the process of being repaired. I could make out minute yachts far away at the northern end of Bassenthwaite Lake, while closer to hand were the carpets of purple heather which adorned the lower reaches of the Edge. Once down at Ravenstone, I found a good path through the woods which took me back to my starting-point and so completed an excellent round on a perfect day. A few months ago I would have regarded this route as a full day's outing, yet here I was in good heart after completing it in just three and a half hours and feeling that I had given myself an easy day. There seems little doubt that the challenge I have set myself is doing me a power of good.

Next day did indeed dawn bright and beautiful, and I took the bus to Buttermere. It was a Sunday in August and Buttermere was bursting at the seams, with people queueing up to buy pay and display tickets for their cars and large groups of hikers assembling for organized rambles. Yet during the course of a long day's walking, and with one notable exception, I encountered only a sprinkling of people, confirming me in my long-held view that, if you are prepared to climb, you can escape the holiday crowds easily enough.

I took the path to Scale Force, enjoying as I went the lovely contrast between the blue of Crummock Water, the green of Rannerdale Knotts and the purple bulk of Grasmoor. A red rock staircase led me up beside Scale Beck to the slimy four-foot rock slab of which Wainwright speaks in his chapter on Red Pike and which had been preying on my mind somewhat. In fact, it is easily passed by a little detour to the left and soon I was making the long, steep climb from the beck up to Lingcomb Edge. From there, the ascent of Red Pike was a simple matter, in stark contrast to my first ascent of it some years earlier, when I approached it by way of Bleaberry Tarn and ended up scrambling up the Saddle on my hands and knees. That was certainly an experience, but one I had no wish to repeat.

From Red Pike I continued to High Stile, where I stopped for a while to absorb the spectacular views north over Red Pike, Mellbreak, Crummock Water and Loweswater. On setting off once more I became disorientated and found myself following a line of cairns which led me not towards my next objective, High Crag, but to a point overlooking the sheer cliffs of Grey Crag. It came as a surprise to find that the ridge I wanted was in fact running away almost due south behind me. I retraced my steps, telling myself as I did so that I really must make more use of my compass even when, as today, the visibility was good. With High Crag now firmly in my sights, I encountered no further problems, though the subsequent descent by way of Gamlin End was as fierce as I remembered it, even allowing for the rock staircase which nowadays makes the lower part of it a great deal easier.

Next came a thoroughly enjoyable ascent of Haystacks, involving a little simple scrambling, and soon I had my fourth fell of the day. Haystacks is clearly a favourite with everyone, Wainwright included, from the age of five upwards and today was no exception. I didn't linger, since I still had one fell - Fleetwith Pike - left to climb, but I made the mistake of leaving the good path I was following much too early and so found myself blazing a trail over undulating terrain covered in tussocky grass. In itself, this was not a problem - all I had to do was keep climbing and I would reach the summit eventually -

but it made this final ascent much tougher than it need have been. As a result, I was just about on my last legs by the time the top of Fleetwith Pike came into view.

Thinking about it since, I realize that I have a marked reluctance to consult maps, or a compass for that matter, whenever I think I know my route. This is particularly true when I get beyond a certain point of tiredness: it simply becomes too much effort to rummage in my pack for the relevant items. This, of course, is daft and something I must try to resist in future, before it gets me into serious trouble.

The view from the summit of Fleetwith Pike along Buttermere to Crummock Water was as lovely as ever, but this time I did not linger. Instead I took the clear track leading down to the dismantled tramway and from there made my way back to Honister Hause. It was blissful to feel tarmac under my feet once more after six and a half hours of loose rock and stone, and half an hour later I was at Seatoller, with just enough time to polish off an iced lolly before catching the bus back to Keswick. This had turned out to be a really taxing walk and one that I had seriously underestimated, imagining that it would take me five hours or less to complete. Given that the total distance was only twelve miles, a time of seven hours represented my slowest rate of progress on any walk to date. I promised myself that tomorrow would be a rest day or at most a very easy outing.

As it turned out, the weather next day was too good for resting, so I opted for a gentle walk over Knott and Great Calva in the northern fells, which afforded me the luxury of grass underfoot the whole way. The blue of the sky, the purple of the heather and the fresh green of the bracken made a wonderfully colourful scene, which was perfectly complemented by the long views to the Pennines, the Mull of Galloway and the Isle of Man. Above all the absolute tranquillity that accompanied me throughout made of this a memorable excursion.

On the final day, I set off from Grasmere with Tarn Crag as my initial objective. My plan was to climb it by the east ridge, but I was unfamiliar with the entire area and arrived at Easedale Tarn without having seen any sign of the path that supposedly turned off on my right and led to the ridge. I reverted to plan B, which was to take Wainwright's route running more or less north from the edge of the tarn and so join the east ridge that way. With this in mind, I skirted the entire northern side of the tarn but nowhere amongst the waist-high bracken could I find any sign of a path.

Time for plan C. This involved continuing round the tarn till I rejoined the main path leading up to Belles Knott. From there I would see if a route to Tarn Crag was discernable on the ground. In Wainwright's day there was nothing. "Tarn Crag," he writes, "is not often visited." Things have changed since he wrote those words. Nowadays there is a clear path, doubtless beaten by all those, like me, bent on doing the Wainwrights. If it meanders in an apparently aimless fashion, it is only because the terrain forbids a direct approach to the summit, but it leads the patient walker there without exposing him to the worst of the marshy ground.

By now the weather was starting to deteriorate and I considered settling for this one fell and returning to Grasmere by the east ridge which had eluded me on the way up. Once again, however, I could find no sign of a clear path running in the direction I wanted. I decided to keep my options open by returning to Belles Knott, from where I could either tackle other fells or, if the weather deteriorated further, return to Grasmere by the way I had come.

When the time came to decide, the cloud was streaming in from the north-west and it seemed to me that this was not the day for exploring unfamiliar fells. I made the direct descent to Grasmere and am very glad I did, for the rain, which had been threatening for some time, came on when I was about three-quarters of a mile from the village and continued steadily for the rest of the day.

I could not help wondering, as I furled my umbrella and climbed wearily into the car, how a group of three walkers I had passed at the top of Sourmilk Gill were getting on. They too were heading back to Grasmere, but slowly, which was understandable given that one of them, an immaculately dressed woman of uncertain age, was wearing very smart high-heeled boots. I had been astonished to see her up by Easedale Tarn, but how she managed the quite rough descent in pouring rain I have no idea.

For my part I was happy to be on my way home. It was true that the weather and general fatigue had restricted me to just three fells over the final two days of my visit, but even so my grand total now stood at one hundred and twenty-six fells and it was more than time to take a rest.

Chapter Ten

September

THERE WAS only one place to be in the Lake District on 10 September and that was on the slopes of Lonscale Fell to watch the World Masters (i.e. veterans) fell-running championships, with eleven hundred and nine entries from twenty-seven countries, including New Zealand and Nigeria! I certainly wanted to be there to catch the action, but I also wanted to get more fells under my belt and had in mind a round taking in Lonscale Fell, Skiddaw Little Man, Skiddaw and Bakestall.

The problem was how to be in the right place at the right time, given that the first race set out from Keswick at 11am and the last at 3.30pm. In view of my own age, I had something of a vested interest in the first three races, for over-seventies, over-sixty-fives and over-sixties respectively. On the other hand, I wanted to see the swiftest exponents of this, to my mind, semi-suicidal activity in action, which meant seeing the over-forties race, due to start at 3.30 pm. Could I somehow combine all these requirements into one perfectly orchestrated day, or would I be on Lonscale Fell too early for the morning races and get back there too late for the afternoon ones? I spent a long time wrestling with the problem before deciding that it was intractable and that the best thing I could do was to set off when I was ready and see what happened.

I duly left Threlkeld at 8.55am and made my way to the Gale Road car park between Skiddaw and Latrigg. Now I was on the route that the fell-runners would take. Climbing the lower slopes of Jenkin Hill, down which many of the competitors would hurtle later in the day, I was struggling, even though the surface of the path had been much improved since I was last there. My pack, with a newly-purchased and supposedly waterproof jacket in it, felt incredibly heavy and it was all I could do to plod up to the point at which the path to Lonscale Fell bears off to the right. This path was marked all the way to the summit, and it later transpired that the fell-runners, having climbed Lonscale Fell from the south, would take this route on their descent to the car-park.

I found myself on the top of Lonscale Fell at 10.35, which of course was far too early, so I promptly turned around and made my way to Skiddaw Little Man. In something of a gale I sat there on a prominent point with binoculars at the ready, hoping to be able to observe the over-seventies from afar. After about fifteen minutes I saw signs of activity on the track below Gale Road, but such was the distance that it was hard to tell who were the competitors and who the spectators. I was still trying to sort them out when low cloud intervened and wiped the entire scene from view, at which point I decided to cut my losses, press on with my walk and hope that I could be back in time to catch the afternoon races.

I made the final ascent of Skiddaw and almost the entire descent to Bakestall in thick mist. On most fells this would have given me cause for concern, but the tracks on Skiddaw are more like motorways and for the descent to Bakestall there is a fence to follow, so I felt happy to proceed. Even so, it was a relief when I finally emerged from the mist and was able to get my bearings visually.

From Bakestall it was a steep and straight descent over grass to the track leading to Skiddaw House. With one eye on the time, I sped along the track, past Skiddaw House and along the eastern flank of Lonscale Fell, reaching its southern face in good time for the first race of the afternoon. The next two and a half hours were spent spectating in warm sunshine. I was full of admiration for the competitors, every one of whom, in my view, deserved a medal. Amazingly, many of them found the breath to say thank-you to me as I stood there politely clapping them on their way. I saw one competitor take a headlong tumble on the steep path down from Jenkin Hill. He was promptly helped to his feet by two fellow-competitors - this in a world championship event! It was a moment which encapsulated everything admirable about this fine sport and its practitioners.

Eventually it was time to make my way back to Threlkeld. My legs, which had been fine while I was hurrying back from Bakestall, now felt incredibly tired and the ball of my right foot was extremely tender. Despite the fact that I was walking downhill all the way, it took me as long to cover this final section as it had at the start of the day when I was going uphill. Subsequent calculations revealed that I had covered fifteen and three-quarter miles in just under six and a half hours, so perhaps it was not surprising that I felt so tired. But then I had four fells and a marvellous afternoon's spectating to show for it.

By next day my legs were still feeling very tired, but the forecast was good so I decided on a route which offered gentle gradients all the way plus much-needed grass underfoot. My starting-point was the car-park above Dowthwaitehead, where I discovered a tent, a row of porta-loos and several cars. It turned out that the National Deaf Children's Society was holding a challenge event - twenty-four fells in twenty-four hours for teams of four - and that this was their finishing-point. This certainly gave me pause for thought. Could I have tackled such an event? Well, maybe in my hey-day forty years ago, but certainly not now. I had only to reflect on how I was feeling after just four fells in twenty-four hours to have no illusions on that score.

Suitably humbled, I set off on my own private and extremely modest challenge, aiming to climb just four fells, or five if you count Birkett Fell, which was my first "summit". As the Ordnance Survey map makes clear, it is not really a fell at all, but an outlying spur of Hart Side, which is doubtless why Wainwright does not include it amongst his Lakeland fells. Nonetheless it has a fine cairn boasting a stone plaque with the name of the fell engraved on it, which few others have.

Here a navigational problem presented itself. My next objective was Hart Side, which according to the map was south-west of Birkett Fell. But the map also showed a feature called Hart Crag lying due west of Birkett Fell and which appeared to be appreciably higher than the area marked Hart Side. As there was a clear path leading over to this Hart Crag, I decided to explore it anyway, before going on to Hart Side. On reaching the highest point just short of the crags, I found that I was in fact on the summit of Hart Side as described by Wainwright, the ditch which ran across the summit leaving no room for doubt. So what the Ordnance Survey map calls Hart Side is really something different, namely the ground rising towards what Wainwright calls Green Side and the map calls White Stones. At which point the layman may be forgiven if he feels somewhat confused.

Fortunately, the situation on the ground was a lot clearer, for a distinct path led from the summit on which I stood all the way to Stybarrow Dodd and from there over Watson's Dodd and Great Dodd and so back to the car-park above Dowthwaitehead. Towards the end of this route I passed several people coming in the opposite direction who said "Well done", evidently in the belief that I was part of the challenge event. I confess that I did not disillusion them but stepped out in style, completing my little route of just over ten miles in four hours and feeling, somewhat to my surprise, that I had recovered from yesterday's efforts in the process.

On waking next morning I knew, even before I started, that it was going to be a hard day. It was not just that I was planning two separate walks on one day, but that my first target was Yewbarrow, overlooking Wast Water. From what I had read about it in Wainwright, I was not at all sure that I would be able to make it to the summit. It is a fell not unlike Mellbreak, which caused me so many problems back in April - long, narrow, very steep-sided and with access largely restricted to the craggy north and south ends. Given that the northern approach sounded completely beyond me, I had somehow to negotiate the scarcely less daunting southern one.

I parked at Overbeck Bridge and set off, full of trepidation. It was a glorious, sunny day and the scenery was stunning, but my first close-up view of Yewbarrow, with the pinnacle of Bell Rib towering into the sky, confirmed that I was in for a hard time. Ahead of me were some half a dozen people and I willed them to take the route which I would have to follow, climbing up by Dropping Crag to reach Great Door. Not one of them did. Clearly, if I was going to do this climb, I would have to do it on my own, without the reassurance of company and without the benefit of anyone else's experience, apart from Wainwright's, that is. But then he obviously revelled in the whole excursion.

I reached the point at which the paths diverge, left for the Over Beck valley, right for Dropping Crag and Great Door. Feeling not unlike a man going to his execution, I turned right. The climb to the foot of Dropping Crag was steep but manageable, but when I reached the gully which I had to negotiate if I was to proceed any further I found myself confronted by rocks offering no obvious way up. The ensuing scramble was quite tricky, and several times I had to reverse gingerly on finding that I could not lever myself up the next bit of rock. This was not my scene at all. More than once I considered abandoning the attempt, but the briefest glance over my shoulder was enough to convince me that that was not a viable option. Somehow or other I had to go up.

And then, quite suddenly, the awkward section was over, though it had lasted long enough to convince me that under no circumstances would I choose to descend by this route. The path now became much easier and I began to think that I had stumbled upon a wimp's cop-out, for it seemed to be by-passing the most craggy parts. But then, no less suddenly, it brought me out at Great Door, just as Wainwright says: "At the top of the gully, on an open slope, climb half-right to reach the ridge exactly, suddenly and dramatically at Great Door: a thrilling moment." Evidently I had been following the main path after all.

The remainder of the climb to the summit, though steep and airy, was simple by comparison and soon I was celebrating my one hundred and thirty-fifth fell. I made quite an occasion of it, perching my pack on the top of the cairn with bright orange pack-liner, trusty umbrella and walking-pole all in evidence and proceeded to photograph it from a variety of angles in celebration of this famous victory over my own misgivings. Then it was time to think about how I would get back down.

Wainwright's description of the descent by the north ridge - "The north ridge route … drops steeply and sharply down a series of rocky cracks in the crag for a few desperate minutes" - was more than enough to deter me from trying it, so I was very happy to avoid Stirrup Crag entirely by taking a path which slants down left from the depression beyond the summit. There are evidently plenty of wimps who share my mindset, for this path, if not exactly eroded by continuous wear and tear, was certainly well used. I planned to join the path which runs down the valley to Overbeck Bridge, but in the event kept too high and ended up having to make a steep but safe descent near Dropping Crag.

Shortly afterwards I celebrated with a blissful lunch-stop overlooking Wast Water and relaxed fully for the first time. It was early afternoon, the sun was hot and Wast Water looked incredibly inviting. I was sorely tempted to call it a day as far as the fells were concerned and to settle for an afternoon of swimming and sun-bathing. But that, I reflected, would mean making the long drive to Wasdale (a round trip of a hundred miles) all over again in order to do the other walk I had in mind for today. With more than one regretful glance at that glorious sheet of blue water, I clambered into the car and drove to Greendale. Fifteen minutes after getting off Yewbarrow I was climbing once more.

Two walks in a day, even on quite modest fells, are hard on the legs, for the amount of ascent and descent involved is so much greater than on most ridge routes. Certainly I found the climb up Middle Fell very hard work indeed. It was not that the terrain was difficult, but that I was climbing yet again. Indeed it felt as though I was climbing for hours, for Middle Fell is one of those infuriating fells which offers the walker one false summit after another, and this under a sun which seemed to be getting hotter all the time. I kept stopping to give my legs a rest and even took to sitting on any rock I happened to pass that was a) near the path and b) flat enough to be comfortable. When eventually I made it to the summit, I found that it had taken me an hour to cover the one and a half miles involved.

I had a good long sit-down on the top, taking in the views over Yewbarrow (I've been up that fearsome route, right to the top!), Wasdale Head, Scafell and Scafell Pike. Then I made my way to Seatallan by an easy route, easy that is until the final climb, on grass to be sure, but oh so steep! My thigh muscles were screaming in protest and I had to stop every twenty metres or so to gasp for breath, but eventually I made it to the top.

Mercifully my last fell of the day, Buckbarrow, involved a long, gradual descent. It seemed odd to be descending in order to climb a fell, but given the state of my legs I was not going to complain about that. Having tracked down the summit - one rocky outcrop amongst many - I remained there for some time, captivated by the sheer scale of the Wasdale Screes opposite me as they rose almost vertically out of Wast Water. Then I descended to the road and made my way back to Greendale, arriving weary but pleased that I had managed to resist temptation and complete the two routes I had planned. I found later that I had been out on the fells for almost seven hours but had covered just ten and a quarter miles. But what miles they had been! For this particular wimp, the day had been a truly memorable experience.

Next day was always going to be, by comparison, a low-key affair, and so it proved. I tackled two minor fells, Holme Fell and Black Fell, north of Coniston. The paths were good and, even on a relatively poor day with a lot of cloud and some rain, the views were excellent, particularly from Black Fell, which may be modest in height but which is strategically situated. Indeed, Wainwright lists no fewer than eight lakes and tarns which are visible from the top. I incorporated a circuit of one of them, the lovely Tarn Hows, into my route, observing plenty of evidence here as on Black Fell of the havoc wrought by the January storm. Then it was back to the car, my legs making it perfectly clear that they had done quite enough, thank you very much, and no, they were not remotely interested in adding Lingmoor Fell to the day's tally.

When I woke next morning they were still extremely reluctant to move and it was all I could do to prise myself out of bed. All the same, I drove to Loweswater intent on climbing the three fells which had eluded me in June, when they had been hidden by low cloud. This time, the weather was overcast and extremely blustery but visibility was not a problem, so I set off for Burnbank Fell, following the course of Holme Beck and looking for a path on my right which would take me to the top. Eventually I came upon what seemed to be a swathe cut through the bracken and heading in the right direction. It looked well trodden so I followed it. Here and there at intervals were bits of blue hose, apparently discarded at random. It was only towards the top of the climb that it finally dawned on me that they were marking a fell-running route (the Loweswater Show was in a few days' time) and that I was on it. No wonder I was struggling with the gradient! The thought of actually running up it, or down it for that matter, was … unthinkable.

Up on Burnbank Fell there was a stiff north-westerly blowing, so I pulled on more clothes and kept on the move, passing over the summits of Blake Fell and Gavel Fell, which were my other two objectives. At this point I decided to extend my route by taking in Great Borne and Starling Dodd as well. I was not at all sure how this plan would work out on the ground, but in fact route-finding proved to be a simple matter - it was just a case of following the right combination of fences all the way.

However, I did encounter one problem immediately after crossing the Flautern Pass path, and that was when I had to choose between negotiating a fence topped with barbed wire (and no stile in sight) or what looked like an impassable bog. I tried the fence first, then the bog and finally, in desperation, opted for the fence once more, risking my manhood in the process. Somehow or other I got over it intact, after which the rest of the walk was without incident. I added Great Borne and Starling Dodd to my collection, before descending to Mosedale by Scale Beck. As I walked back to Loweswater, I looked around me and realized that I had climbed every fell in sight. It was a good feeling and a nice note on which to leave the Lake District, with a grand total of one hundred and forty-five fells behind me.

Chapter Eleven

Fund-raising

FROM THE VERY beginning, the idea of doing the Wainwrights was linked in my mind with raising money for M.E. North-East. M.E. stands for Myalgic Encephalomyelitis, a condition which also goes by the name of Chronic Fatigue Syndrome or sometimes Post-Viral Fatigue Syndrome. Typically it involves cripplingly low energy levels, both mental and physical, accompanied by a host of other symptoms which vary from one individual to another. Early diagnosis undoubtedly improves the chances of recovery, provided that sufferers are prepared to take the measures necessary to conserve such depleted energy levels as they possess. However, roughly one in four will be severely affected long-term and, as luck would have it, my wife Jen was one of these.

She developed M.E. after a viral illness when she was thirty-six, our elder daughter not yet three and our younger daughter not even a twinkle in the eye. Since then, we have all of us had to learn to live with it. Some twenty years on, Jen now needs a wheelchair to get about outside the house, which is why she is unable to accompany me on any of my fell-walking expeditions, though that has not stopped her from being marvellously supportive of the whole scheme.

In those far-off, bad old days when M.E. first surfaced in our lives, it was dismissed as 'yuppie flu', something that was 'all in the mind'. If you really wanted to get better, so this philosophy went, all you had to do was snap out of your lethargy and get on with life, which many did or tried to do, with devastating consequences. Over the years, there has been a sea-change in attitudes and a general acceptance that the condition is a real one requiring careful management if it is not to escalate. Nevertheless, an understanding of what causes it is still some way off, while an effective cure or range of cures - for it presents a huge variety of symptoms - is not on the horizon. Sufferers - it is estimated that there are about two hundred and forty thousand in the UK - need a lot of support in learning about M.E. and how best to cope with it.

It can affect people of any age, a fact that we were reminded of most painfully when Hannah, our elder daughter, developed it while studying for her GCSEs. Fortunately, there was a quick diagnosis and a lot of experience within our household of how to deal with it, and in due course she made a full recovery.

Given this family history of ours, the choice of M.E. North-East (we live in Northumberland) as the charity for which I wanted to raise funds was an obvious one. Then came the events related in the opening chapter of this book, which left me with a feeling of profound gratitude towards the British Heart Foundation, whose freely available booklets about virtually every aspect of heart disease were a huge help in dealing with what was at the time a very scary experience. Consequently, when I began thinking once more about doing the Wainwrights, I felt that I would like to divide whatever money I could raise between these two charities.

It could be argued that, after the prostate cancer, I should have extended my choice of charities to three. Certainly the thought crossed my mind, but I decided against it on the grounds that I was already proposing to divide by two what might well turn out to be quite a small sum of money.

I was a bit anxious about the fund-raising side of things. Never having done anything like this before, I was not at all sure how to go about it. Then it occurred to me that a good way might be to invite people to sponsor me at so much per fell. The M.E. North-East office kindly produced tailor-made sponsorship forms which spelled out how much potential sponsors would be committing themselves to, anywhere on a scale from one to ten pence per fell. The idea seemed to catch on and people signed up to the scheme at rates ranging right up to twenty pence per fell which, if I managed to climb all two hundred and fourteen, would mean a donation of £42-80. My sister in Australia trumped the lot by sponsoring me at two dollars per fell, which I later discovered meant just over £177 in real money.

When I first came up with this idea of sponsorship, I imagined that it would help to spur me on when the going got tough, knowing that the summit just ahead of me would bring in another x pounds for two causes I really cared about. In practice, though, it never worked out like that. This was in part because the fund-raising exercise proved so protracted that it lasted almost as long as the fell-walking itself. Besides, pledges came in all sorts of guises, including Australian dollars and Cypriot cents. And then there were those people who preferred to sponsor me for a fixed sum of their choice, regardless of the number of fells climbed. Now while this was very welcome - after all, if I broke a leg on my first day out, sponsorship per fell would not amount to very much - their donations rarely divided easily by 214. Being no mathematician, I soon gave up on the idea of knowing precisely what each summit represented in cash terms. If the going got tough, I would have to settle for the notion that a sum unspecified hung on my reaching the top, and if that did not work then I would have to look elsewhere for the necessary inspiration.

Given that I was pretty busy throughout the year climbing the fells, I did not have a great deal of time to devote to fund-raising. I distributed sponsorship forms as and where I could and leafleted every house in my village. Family and friends across the globe were canvassed and I produced interim progress reports for the Hexham Courant as well as for the publications of M.E. North-East and the British Heart Foundation, but that was as much as I could manage. Considering how low-profile was the publicity and how relatively restricted was the group of people I could reach, I was surprised to find that, by the autumn of 2005, over a hundred households had signed up to the scheme. That was really heartening and left me more resolved than ever to deliver on the fell-walking front. With the leafleting finished, it was time to pull on my boots once more.

Chapter Twelve

October

I RETURNED to the Lake District at the beginning of October, feeling under a certain amount of pressure. I still had sixty-nine fells to climb and I knew that, after this visit, I would not be back again till November, by which time I could hardly expect the weather to be in my favour. Also the clocks would have gone back, so that hours of daylight would be in short supply. It followed that I needed to make the most of this visit to tick off as many fells as I possibly could. This applied particularly to those fells which were difficult of access, high and exposed or unfamiliar to me, which seemed to cover just about all the remaining sixty-nine. I was obviously going to have some hard decisions to make and some taxing walks to do.

I opened my campaign in Grasmere. The plan was to climb Silver How, Blea Rigg and Sergeant Man, followed by Pavey Ark and the three Langdale Pikes, after which I would return to Grasmere via Easedale Tarn. The merit of this scheme was that, if successfully completed, it would spare me the need to make a trip to the Langdale valley specifically to climb the Langdale Pikes. The drawback, as I came to appreciate in due course, was that it was hugely ambitious.

The climb up Silver How from the little boating centre on Grasmere was delightful and the view from the top was quite wonderful. Grasmere and Rydal Water were spread out below me, perfect mirrors with not a ripple to disturb their surfaces. On the fells around them, swathes of low-level, misty cloud hung almost motionless, leaving the tops clear and lending a particularly atmospheric quality to the scene. What a start to the walk!

From Silver How I set off on a path that meandered, dipping and climbing, all the way to Blea Rigg. The route was clear and I was never in danger of losing it, but progress was slow, for the rock underfoot required care. There had obviously been a great deal of rain since I was last in the Lake District - there was a lot of surface water in evidence and the peat-hags were decidedly squishy - and as a result the rocks were frequently very greasy.

Along the way I came upon a small tarn which in itself was unremarkable, but which offered such a perfect reflection of a rocky outcrop overlooking it and of the sky above that it was more than I could do to pass it by without attempting to capture it on camera. More camera-work was called for at Blea Rigg. From here I had fine views north and south over a succession of ridges, each of them dusted with a sprinkling of misty, white cloud, which was constantly forming, dispersing and re-forming elsewhere, so that the scene was ever-changing.

Next came Sergeant Man, the first fell I had been obliged to climb twice. However, I did not in the least mind about this second ascent, for the first had seemed rather a cheat, involving a downhill walk from High Raise. This time I climbed it properly - i.e. from below - before going on to Pavey Ark in persistent drizzle. Here I scaled the three highest points I could see, but found no summit cairn - has it been destroyed since Wainwright's time or did the true summit elude me in the intermittent mist?

A well-timed lunch-stop at this point allowed me to review the situation. The route thus far had taken me much longer than expected and, if I was to do all that I planned, it would probably entail some ten hours of walking. Clearly this grand scheme of mine was altogether too grand. That being so, there seemed little point in climbing Harrison Stickle, my next objective, since

I would have to return at some later date to climb the other two Langdale Pikes. Better surely to do all three together on another occasion and to make my way back to Grasmere now. So I reasoned, but the fact that Harrison Stickle loomed up ahead of me, grey and forbidding when it was not entirely concealed by cloud, certainly had something to do with my decision. I turned back.

There was a magical moment on my return journey when a flock of wild geese passed overhead in a very long and rather ragged V-formation, uttering their unmistakable cries as they flew south-west. I felt pretty ragged too by the time I reached Grasmere, so it was just as well I had curtailed my expedition. Even so, I had been out on the fells for nearly seven and a half hours, though my tally for the day, given that I had climbed Sergeant Man before, amounted to just three fells. To say that they were hard-won is an under-statement.

Next day, I set off from Great Langdale, hoping that the low-level cloud which was still a feature of the weather would not be a problem as I tackled three more unfamiliar fells, Pike o'Blisco, Cold Pike and Crinkle Crags. The path up Pike o'Blisco - a rock staircase much of the way - was steep but easy to follow. Apart from one brief scramble over some rather slimy-looking rock, it was a straightforward climb and I reached the impressive summit-cairn exactly two hours after setting off.

By now the patches of cloud had lifted and visibility remained good for the rest of the day. I took in the view and visited the secondary cairn but my main concern was to find out what awaited me on the western side of Pike o'Blisco. To my relief, I found that the path was clearly visible all the way to the distant Crinkle Crags, so there would be no navigational problems. I descended to Red Tarn, made a simple detour to Cold Pike, and then headed for the Crinkles.

These I thoroughly enjoyed, even peering down some of the ravines, albeit from positions of absolute safety. The bad step on the second Crinkle, about which I had entertained some anxiety, is in fact very obvious when seen from below. I avoided it with ease, veering left on a well-beaten path which took me to the summit without incident. Having reached the top of this the highest Crinkle, I had strictly speaking "done" this fell, but I nonetheless took great delight in visiting the tops of all three remaining Crinkles. However, I was disconcerted to find that even after that there were still two further tops, going by the name of Shelter Crags, between me and my turning-off point for Great Langdale. After negotiating these, I made the long, steep descent down the Band, much of it on more stone staircases. It took a full hour to reach the valley, then it was back along the road to the car, enjoying the magnificent views, particularly of the Langdale Pikes as they rise so dramatically from the valley floor. Sooner or later, and preferably before winter set in, I would need to tackle them.

And so next day saw me, contrary to my normal practice, back in Great Langdale with my sights set this time on those Langdale Pikes. From New Dungeon Ghyll I took the rock staircase which goes all the way up to Pike How, an excellent viewpoint. From there Harrison Stickle looked forbidding, with no obvious way up it at all. I pressed on towards the huge rock-face ahead of me, uncomfortably aware that, while other routes to the Langdales were visibly busy, my route was utterly deserted.

Had I inadvertently chosen the toughest route of all? I recalled what Wainwright has to say about the latter stages of this climb: "This steep scree slope above the ravine is loose. Except for the path, nothing is firm." While gearing myself up for what might lie ahead, I was already preparing plan B. This involved backtracking to a point where I could take a path east to Stickle Tarn. From there I would attempt to find a way up, if necessary walking right round the eastern flank of Pavey Ark in the process. In short, I was prepared to do anything rather than expose myself to a hair-raising ascent up a loose scree-slope above a ravine.

As I approached the part of the route in question, with the ravine falling away to my left, the path began to thread its way in between and over huge slabs of rock. I scrambled on, convinced that at any moment it would swing to the right and there before me would be the dreaded scree-slope. But no - the path emerged onto flat grass with no scree in sight! So much for my unwarranted apprehension and my unnecessary plan B. Hugely relieved, I set about the final climb to the summit with gusto, positively revelling in the easy scrambling involved, and soon I was atop Harrison Stickle, sharing the summit only with a raven.

My next target was Pike o'Stickle and on a clear day such as this there was no mistaking the pyramid of rock, thrusting up from the grassy plateau on which it stands. Even from a distance it was obvious that the only way to the top involved a steep scramble. Would I make it or would this be the first fell to deny me its summit? As I approached, I was staggered to see two sheep perched on minuscule patches of grass near the summit, grazing as blissfully as if they were in some vast meadow rather than on a precipice with a fall of at least fifteen hundred feet immediately beneath them.

I kept to the path till there was no option but to grapple with the rock-face. For the space of about ten metres the climb was rather too testing for comfort, with hand- and foot-holds not always readily available, but after that it was plain sailing. Standing on the top I enjoyed the view back to Harrison Stickle, then scrambled down to the path by what turned out to be an easier route than my way up. A few minutes later I was on top of Loft Crag, the last of the Langdale Pikes. There I had lunch and watched in disbelief as two fell-runners jogged down the path beside the ravine which had caused me so much apprehension on my way up Harrison Stickle.

October

From Loft Crag the route back down to Dungeon Ghyll was good, the scree of which Wainwright speaks having been avoided by yet another excellent stone staircase. By 3pm I was back in the valley, tired but happy. The Langdale Pikes were in the bag.

However, there was still unfinished business ahead of me and that was Lingmoor Fell, just across the valley from where I stood. It was the only one of the southern fells that I had still to climb. Was I really going to leave it unscaled when the weather was good and I had ample time to do it? Of course not, I told my protesting legs, and set off up the Wall End road. Ever the wimp, I took the road because the path which Wainwright recommends had a lot of cattle on it or near it.

Lingmoor Fell proved to be an absolute delight. The path was clear all the way to the top and included some easy and enjoyable scrambling. The sun was out and beneath me Blea Tarn sparkled like a giant diamond. However, the true summit proved to be much further on than I had thought, being preceded by that bane of the weary fell-walker, the false summit, and in this case not one but two of them. A brief rest on the true top confirmed me in the impression that this was a fell I wanted to revisit in order to explore it at greater leisure.

For now, though, I could not linger. I could actually make out my car far away near Chapel Stile, but at right angles to the route I had taken to reach this point. I had of necessity to take the same route back, since I was far from sure that I could find another which would take me in the direction of my car. So back I went to Dungeon Ghyll and from there to Chapel Stile, knowing that over the last two days I had fallen in love with Greater Langdale and would certainly be back once the Wainwrights were all behind me. And how strange that, of all the Wainwright volumes, the first to be finished should be that devoted to the southern fells, which for so long had lagged behind all the others.

Doing the Wainwrights

On my final day, the forecast was for a lot of low cloud, so I drove to Troutbeck, east of Ambleside, with a view to climbing four outlying fells. En route, the top of Kirkstone Pass had been swathed in thick mist and it was not long before I was back in more of the same as I climbed from Troutbeck up towards Sallows. I was also more than a little damp, for this was what the Irish call a soft day.

Eventually I left the stony track I had been following and took a path which led me over moorland to the summit. Without the path I would never have found it, for in the thick mist I could not see more than a few metres in any direction, and the summit is just a small mound with no cairn and not much in the way of distinguishing features. Comparison with Wainwright's drawing and description enabled me to identify it, after which I retraced my steps, or rather attempted to. In point of fact I missed a junction and ended up at the stone wall which separates Sallows from its neighbour, Sour Howes, which was my next objective.

There was a stile so I clambered over, assuming that, with the benefit of this unintentional short cut, I would soon be at the summit. In fact it took me a further thirty-five minutes to locate it. The summit of Sour Howes, like that of Sallows, is quite inconspicuous and is moreover surrounded by a host of other mounds, any one of which could be mistaken for the top in thick mist like this. Height, like distance, seems to be magnified by mist, so that time and again I climbed a hillock full of hope that it was the top, only to find that it bore no resemblance whatever to Wainwright's description. One way and another I was heartily glad when I had finally located the top and could return to the car where at least I had some sort of a view.

The weather had not improved by the time I had had my lunch, but I felt obliged to set off in search of my third objective, Wansfell, on the opposite side of the Troutbeck valley from Sallows and Sour Howes. It was not long before I was back in the mist. Turning off Nanny Lane I again placed my faith in a narrow path which took me over one hillock after another, each of which, it seemed to me, had to be the summit. After numerous disappointments I eventually reached the true summit and here I took a gamble.

Originally, I had intended to retrace my steps as the only safe way back in mist, but I allowed myself to be beguiled by a well-tramped path ahead of me which I believed would return me to Nanny Lane more directly than the route by which I had come. The further this new path ran on the more I began to doubt the wisdom of my decision, especially when I found myself crossing a boggy patch where I could feel the surface flexing beneath my feet. I kept peering to my left for signs of the wall that would indicate that I was nearing Nanny Lane, expecting to see it appear out of the mist at any minute. Instead, to my utter consternation a wall eventually appeared on my right.

I consulted my maps and Wainwright. Could this be the ridge wall heading for Wansfell Pike? Or - a thought occasioned by a brief downhill stretch - was I already beyond that point and heading for Ambleside? Certainly the compass told me that I was going south, whereas Troutbeck lay east. I decided to persevere a little longer in the knowledge that, if the worst came to the worst, I could always - I hoped - retrace my steps to the summit of Wansfell. I was pondering what I would do on reaching the boggy patch once more when a rocky eminence suddenly loomed up out of the mist and I found myself on Wansfell Pike. What a relief! Now at last I knew where I was and I had a good path to follow all the way back to Nanny Lane and so to the car.

By then I had been wandering about in mist for over five hours, with never a view in sight. Quite honestly I had had enough and, abandoning thoughts of tackling Troutbeck Tongue, I headed back to base and from there to home. It was just as well I did, for I felt absolutely shattered for the next two days. In a bid to get as many fells behind me as possible before the onset of winter I had obviously overdone it a bit. But with one hundred and fifty-eight fells climbed and just fifty-six to go I could afford to take it more gently in the future. Perhaps.

Chapter Thirteen

November

IT WAS OVER six weeks before I returned to the Lake District and by then the rules of the game had changed. We were into the second half of November, daylight hours were at a premium and one really needed to be off the fells by 4pm. And of course it was much colder, bitterly cold in fact, with several degrees of frost each night and a lot of ice underfoot by day. There was also ice on the minor roads to contend with and quite a lot of freezing fog too, so that suddenly the outlying fells were doubly difficult of access. I was extremely glad that by now I had all the southern fells, all but one of the central fells and most of the western fells behind me, for the idea of driving into Wasdale or the Langdale valley in those conditions was far from appealing. As for the Wrynose and Hardknott passes, they were both closed to traffic.

The most outlying routes that I had still to do involved starting from Troutbeck in the south and from Buttermere in the west, neither of which would be easy journeys in the circumstances. When it became clear that the weather was not going to change during this stay, I postponed the walk from Troutbeck till a later visit, not wishing to negotiate the Kirkstone pass in the prevailing conditions. As for Buttermere, I planned to get there by bus, only to discover that the buses had stopped running at the end of October and there was no winter service whatever. So that route too would have to wait for more clement weather.

Doing the Wainwrights

Now that I had just fifty-six fells left to climb, there was much less choice available to me on any given day. Indeed, on this first day of my visit there was no choice at all for, having driven across from Northumberland just before lunch, it was after 2pm before I was ready to start. The only route that I could cover in around two and a half hours and that was readily accessible to me was a climb over Carrock Fell and High Pike in the northern fells.

I duly parked at the foot of Carrock Fell and, breaking my rule of allowing myself ten minutes' easy walking before starting to climb, took the direct route up by way of Rake Trod. This was not the wisest thing to do given that the air was bitterly cold. It had been minus six celsius the previous night and even now the ground was covered with hoar-frost down to about twelve hundred feet (365 metres). However, I did not have enough time at my disposal to grant myself the luxury of a gradual warm-up, so to compensate I made a point of taking the climb very steadily, pausing several times on the steep initial section. As it happened, the climb was less of a slithering, scrambling affair than normal, since much of the usually loose surface had frozen into a solid block over which I passed quite easily, and I experienced no chest pain whatever. In forty-five minutes I was on top of Carrock Fell, with High Pike in my sights.

It was just as well that visibility was good, for the first part of the route to High Pike is far from clear. It is also abominably wet, or would have been had it not been so cold. As it was, I waltzed over even the boggiest sections without so much as a squelch and reached High Pike with my feet bone dry.

Then came a brief moment of panic when the top proved to be totally different from the description in Wainwright. Had I climbed the wrong fell? I peered at the map and realized my mistake: the description I had been reading related not to High

Pike but to Great Sca Fell. I had somehow got it into my head that it was the latter I was climbing and so had consulted the wrong chapter.

With that misunderstanding behind me, I made a brisk descent by Carrock Beck with the light fading fast. No matter, for all I had to do was to follow the road back to the car, or so I thought. However, on reaching the point where Carrock Beck flows over the road, I found that the footbridge had disappeared without trace, presumably swept away in the January storm. How was I to get across? There was too much water in the beck for me to simply plodge across on the road, which anyway was covered with ice on either side of the beck and doubtless beneath it too. There was nothing for it: I was going to have to rock-hop across, not an easy matter given that most of the rocks in the beck were themselves covered in ice. After a few false starts I somehow managed to get across dry-shod. By then it was well and truly dark. Still, I had now climbed all the northern fells save Blencathra, which, if all went according to plan, would be the final summit of the whole exercise.

Next day, with dry weather forecast, I drove to Patterdale, for I was anxious to climb the Helvellyn group during this stay if at all possible. As I walked along the road to Glenridding, the view over Ullswater was magical, with mist rising gently from the lake. The surface was absolutely still and formed a perfect mirror, till two mute swans flew across at low-level, beating the water with the full span of their wings as they went. What a marvellous sight with which to start the day!

From Glenridding I took the direct route to Raise, climbing through the old mine-workings and following the course of the long-disused aqueduct. The final part of the climb, pathless and into a bitterly cold head wind, was hard work and, when low cloud closed in, it became quite a task to locate the summit. By now I was in full winter gear and just about keeping warm as the icy wind buffeted me.

From Raise I had to rely on the compass in order to make my way to my next destination, White Side. Finding myself still in cloud once there, I considered abandoning the rest of the route and descending to Glenridding. As I stood havering, the cloud lifted enough to give me a clear view of the path up to Helvellyn. It was almost a motorway, with plenty of other walkers heading up it, so I decided to carry on while keeping open the option of retracing my steps should I find the conditions too unpleasant. In fact, the walking proved to be good, with no ice underfoot, and soon I was on the summit.

By this time, however, the cloud was down again, presenting me with a fresh navigational challenge. Using my compass, I headed south on a good path but realized, when it started descending, that I had by-passed my next objective, Nethermost Pike. I turned back, still in low cloud, and made a detour east to try and find the unobtrusive summit, which eventually I did. Then it was back to the path and onwards to Dollywaggon Pike.

Fearing that I would again by-pass the summit, I turned off the path too early this time, having glimpsed a cairn on top of a rocky prominence on my left. On closer inspection, this proved to be not Dollywaggon Pike, but something else I could not identify. Unable to see what lay ahead if I carried on in the same direction, I returned to my path, congratulating myself on my prudence in doing so. However, when the cloud lifted shortly afterwards I discovered that, had I indeed carried on from the cairn in question, I would have come straight to Dollywaggon Pike. As I made an unnecessarily steep climb to my final summit of the day, I at least had the satisfaction of knowing that I had made the right decision in the circumstances.

From Dollywaggon Pike I descended to Patterdale by way of Grisedale Tarn, taking care to avoid the large patches of ice which occasionally covered the path. By the time I reached the car the light was fading fast, so my decision not to include a further fell, Seat Sandal, in this excursion had definitely been the right one. And once again I had made full use of the hours of daylight. With Helvellyn done, I had now climbed all four Lakeland fells in excess of three thousand feet and had even managed, albeit with a few hiccups along the way, to track down all the day's objectives in low cloud. So one way and another I was feeling pretty pleased with myself as I drove back to base camp.

Next day brought a challenge of a different order. The day was cold, but the skies were clear - perfect conditions for climbing - and I drove to Deepdale Bridge, from where I hoped to climb four or possibly five of the far eastern fells. It was that potential fifth one which set this outing apart from all my previous fell-walking trips, for the fell in question was The Nab, the only one of the Wainwrights where walkers are not welcome. I had read Wainwright on the subject several times and the message was loud and clear: "PLEASE DO NOT INTRUDE." For this fell lies wholly within the Martindale Deer Forest and is a sanctuary for the deer that breed there. No public right of way crosses the fell which, Wainwright points out, is guarded by "Keep out notices, barricaded gates, and miles of barb (sic) wire."

So what is the conscientious fell-walker to do? Wainwright offers two alternatives. One is to seek permission to proceed at the keeper's bungalow but, as this is located well up Rampsgill Beck, it is a major expedition in itself simply to get there and, if permission is refused, all one can do is return to Martindale. The alternative is to follow Wainwright's example and explore the fell surreptitiously, in other words to trespass. Wainwright himself, while clearly uncomfortable about including The Nab, obviously felt unable simply to omit it. There is a note in the chapter on Rest Dodd which encapsulates his dilemma. Alongside a description of the ridge route from Rest Dodd to The Nab, he writes: "These notes and diagrams are given only for the sake of completeness of records; no inducement to trespass is intended."

Doing the Wainwrights

His dilemma extends to all those who, like me, seek to do the Wainwrights. On the one hand, I am extremely uncomfortable with the idea of trespassing. On the other, I am quite desperate not to find myself in the same position as a fell-walker I had met in Keswick who informed me that she had done all the Wainwrights and then added, after a pause, "Well, all except the one that's private." Typically, I set off with the issue undecided in my mind. I would climb Rest Dodd, assess the lie of the land from there and then decide about The Nab.

I climbed by way of Boardale Hause to Angletarn Pikes, the first of my five fells. They offered lovely views west over Patterdale and south over Angle Tarn, which was almost entirely frozen over. After a brief excursion west to my second objective, Brock Crags, I made for Rest Dodd. As it happened, the path I was on swung round to the north-western side of the fell and so brought me in the vicinity of the stone wall I would have to cross if I was going to visit The Nab. At this point, a path made straight for the wall. The moment of truth had arrived.

I stopped and mulled over the situation. I could disregard this path and climb to the summit of Rest Dodd but, if I then decided that I would indeed explore The Nab, I would have to return to where I was now standing. Moreover, I would have to climb much of Rest Dodd a second time after visiting The Nab. This clearly made no sense, so I followed the path through a collapsed section of the wall. I was now trespassing. I just hoped I wouldn't get nabbed!

The path, increasingly indistinct, led me over to the eastern side of the fell, where I found a very well-trodden path - there is clearly no shortage of trespassers - which led all the way to the summit, passing through the most atrocious peat-hags on the way. Fortunately for me they were frozen solid, for in normal circumstances I would have been at least ankle-deep in peat.

November

There was no sign of man or beast as I progressed towards the summit, but that did not stop me from imagining a whole array of scenarios in which an irate gamekeeper leaps from a hide constructed specifically for the purpose of intercepting trespassers and demands to know my name and address with a view to prosecution. Consequently I did not hang about on top of The Nab, but scurried back along my outward path as quickly as the peat-hags would permit. Since this path was heading straight for the boundary wall and was visible beyond as it climbed up to the summit of Rest Dodd, I decided to stick with it rather than veering off to the gap in the wall through which I had come.

My path took me to the point at which the wall begins to plunge down towards Ramps Gill and here, far from being confronted by barricades and barbed wire, I found a stile. I crossed the wall and was a trespasser no longer. Only then did I spot a National Trust notice-board fixed to the Rest Dodd side of the stile. It informed me that The Nab is now open-access land, but that, to avoid disturbing the deer, there is a preferred out-and-back route running directly between this stile and the summit. It was the route I had just taken on my way back. For a moment I felt rather foolish as I recalled my furtiveness, but then I reflected that I now had The Nab under my belt, and legitimately so, meaning that a final target of two hundred and fourteen fells, not two hundred and thirteen, remained distinctly on the cards.

Thus encouraged, I climbed the extremely steep slope up to Rest Dodd, whose summit cairn has these days lost its flagpole, and there I stopped for lunch. The sky was a deep blue, the view in all directions was crystal clear and above all there was absolute stillness - no wind, no sound save for the distant barking of a dog somewhere down in Patterdale. It was a privilege to experience such blissful tranquillity combined with such a beautiful outlook and I savoured the moment.

Then I was on my way once more, dropping down from Rest Dodd before climbing steeply up to The Knott, my last fell of the day. From there I made my way back to Angle Tarn, where I skimmed stones over the ice and listened to the strange, echoing sound they made, not unlike the cries of wild geese in flight.

As I passed below Angletarn Pikes I came upon an unexpected final treat. On the fellside about a hundred metres below me was a herd of ten deer, the first I had ever seen on the open fells of the Lake District. It was as if The Nab had arranged this as a farewell gesture. I watched them grazing and, though they saw me, I was too far away to pose any threat and they carried on peacefully. With the sun dipping behind the fell-tops and the temperature dropping rapidly, I prised myself away and descended to Deepdale Bridge, reflecting on the wonderful day I had had.

When I woke next morning, Blencathra was clear and glowing in the sunlight but, by the time I set off in the car for Braithwaite, it had virtually disappeared in low cloud. My plan was to climb Causey Pike by way of Sleet Hause, but Wainwright's remark about the final rock-tower requiring the use of hands was exercising me a bit, particularly with such a lot of hoar-frost and ice about. On discovering that the Pike was hidden in thick mist, I revised my plans and settled for taking the track up by Stonycroft Gill. That way I could approach it from the west, an easy route which would avoid all the scrambling. It is of course a wimp's way of tackling Causey Pike, but I felt it was justified in the circumstances.

Going up by the gill I was soon in thick, grey mist and I wondered if I would be able to find my way to my objective, even by this easy route. Then, as I climbed, the mist above me gradually turned darker and the next thing I knew I was out under clear blue sky, with the upper part of Causey Pike bathed in sunlight. A well-beaten path left my track and made directly for it, so I followed that. I was out of the mist but still in the shadow of the hillside ahead of me and underfoot all was hoar-frost, and yet I could feel the air getting warmer as I climbed - a most unusual state of affairs! When finally I emerged from the shadow into the sun the air was not just warm but hot. Off came two pairs of gloves, a down jacket and a fleece and I began to think that perhaps I should have brought a sun-hat!

Causey Pike is a giddy sort of place, with the ground falling away sharply on all sides - so sharply towards Sleet Hause that I could not even bring myself to peer over the edge to see what I had avoided. Several hundred feet below me a vast expanse of dazzling white cloud stretched in all directions - far out into the Irish Sea, across to the Pennines and north over the Solway Firth. The landscape was transformed by this white ocean as if by a flood of Biblical proportions. The mountains of the Lake District were now isolated islands, while the lakes, valleys, farms, roads, towns and villages had all disappeared. This new scheme of things made it even clearer than normal which were the fells to be reckoned with and which the also-rans. Skiddaw and Blencathra still rose majestically above the white tide-line, while Dodd, Barf and Catbells were like mini-sandcastles on the brink of being totally submerged.

I walked along the ridge from Causey Pike to Sail by way of Scar Crags, bathed all the way in warm sunshine. The gentlest of breezes was blowing and the world seemed a radiantly beautiful and peaceful place. I sat on Sail and absorbed the whole blissful experience, before making my way down to Outerside. En route I passed from summer to mid-winter as I found myself once more in the shadow of the hillside and so back in the land of hoar-frost and ice.

Outerside itself was in the sun and from its top I enjoyed once more the white ocean and the islands. Then I rejoined the Stonycroft Gill track and descended into the cloud and winter. My last target for the day was Barrow, which I had never climbed before and which was clearly going to be entirely shrouded in mist. Luckily I took the right turning and a good path led me all the way to the summit and from there down to Braithwaite. I saw nothing of the scenery but felt sure that this was a fell worth revisiting.

Back at the car, I peeled off my winter gear and drove home. It had been a day of strange contrasts, but I had managed to climb the five fells I set out to climb and my grand total now stood at one hundred and seventy-five. Thirty-nine to go.

Chapter Fourteen

Base Camp

BASE CAMP in the Lake District is a battered old caravan purchased second-hand many years ago and which in its hey-day gave us some excellent family holidays. Now it has grown old and arthritic and remains glued to the spot, showing all the signs of a decline which in the not too distant future will prove terminal. It leaks, but only moderately, having been glued together over the years with a whole array of adhesive tapes and resinous substances that purport to keep water at bay. Inside, the ceiling and walls display a variety of curves and bulges that testify to the limited success of these remedies. It has a gas hob, parts of which still work, but the only electricity comes by way of an extension lead from the farm's mains supply, so that electric light and heat are possible, but electrically operated pumps for the taps are not. In consequence, all water must be stored in, and poured from, a collection of plastic bottles with which I tangle every time I enter or leave the caravan. Needless to say, there is no shower. On really hot days, one can immerse oneself in the nearby stream. For the other eleven and a half months of the year, a small plastic bowl half-full of warm water is the nearest thing to a bath on offer. There is also no fridge, though perishables can be stored in a freezer-box which in winter is unnecessary and in summer is ineffective, but which nevertheless makes a very good bedside table.

In short, the caravan is by no means luxurious and, like its occupant, is showing its age. This was most graphically illustrated in mid-December 2005 during a spell of bitterly cold weather. Puzzled one morning by the fact that it felt so cold inside the caravan despite having the heating on full-blast, I discovered that the shutter which fits over one of the air-vents in the roof had simply disappeared, leaving a large, square hole open to the elements. Fortunately it had not rained or snowed overnight, so it was only in the morning that I became aware of the problem. Closer inspection revealed that the shutter had snapped clean off. I eventually found it some fifty yards from the caravan, on the far side of a farm out-building. It is a substantial item, so the gust of wind that had presumably caught it must have been fierce indeed. Except that, as I then realized, there had not been any fierce gusts in the night, not that fierce anyway, for I would certainly have felt them. So presumably the shutter had been absent when I arrived the previous evening and I had simply not noticed.

At all events, I had the shutter now and the main thing was to get it back in place before any nasty weather arrived. I cast around for something with which to attach it to the caravan. The only thing I could find was a rather worn bit of string, so I tied it in place with that and at the earliest opportunity replaced the string by garden wire. Like the anti-leaking strategies, it is a Heath-Robinson repair which, with luck, will buy base camp a little more time.

Luxurious it may not be, but it keeps me warm and dry and above all, by its location within the Lake District, makes it feasible for me to tackle the Wainwrights. It and I have survived nights so cold that the gas has frozen solid in the gas bottle (another Heath-Robinson device - sheets of bubble-wrap bound round the bottle - seems to have solved that problem) or so windy that we have rocked together as if on the open sea. We have aged together, developed defects together, but are both still just about in working order.

Base Camp

It remains a good place to which to return at the end of a day's walking. I can brew up as many pints of tea as I want, have a quick wash-down (very quick in winter!), soak my feet in warm water (bliss!), feed myself to bursting-point and then get down to the serious business of writing up the day's walk and planning the route for tomorrow. Then I fall into bed and sleep for anything up to ten hours before starting the process all over again: local weather forecast on Radio Cumbria, revision - sometimes wholesale revision - of yesterday's plans in the light of that information, a phone-call to Jen with details of my route for the day on the understanding that, if I have not been in touch again by a pre-arranged time, there has been a problem and she needs to raise the alarm, and then off on what I hope will be another glorious day on the fells.

Chapter Fifteen

December

THE DAYS WERE shorter still when I returned to the Lake District in mid-December and my top priority was to get to Troutbeck as soon as conditions lent themselves to driving over the Kirkstone Pass. As it happened I was able to do that on my first day, which was clear and cold, but with almost no ice on the road.

From Troutbeck I made my way to Town Head, passing the Mortal Man pub en route and hoping that it was not some sort of omen for what lay ahead. On reaching Troutbeck Park I made a direct ascent of The Tongue, my first fell of the day. A bitterly cold wind was blowing on the top, but the fells all around were crystal clear and Windermere was glinting in the sunlight, so I attempted a few photographs. None of them was much good for the wind was hitting me so hard that, try as I might, I could not hold the camera steady.

I walked the length of Troutbeck Tongue, which offered a fine platform from which to enjoy the surrounding fells, then climbed steeply to the ridge linking Thornthwaite Crag to Froswick. Now I was on a ridge route that I would follow all the way to the Garburn Pass, visiting the summits of Froswick, Ill Bell and Yoke on the way. The walk to the top of Froswick was an easy one on grass, but when Ill Bell came into view it presented a daunting aspect - a dramatic cliff-face crowned by upward-thrusting rocks. Contrary to appearances it proved a thoroughly enjoyable climb, with a good path by-passing the cliffs and threading its way through the rocks to the summit. And what a summit it is, with not one but three fine cairns on it. I sheltered from the wind in the lee of the main one and ate my lunch in comfort and in sunshine - this at almost two and a half thousand feet in mid-December!

From here the route continued easily over Yoke and down to the Garburn Pass. This latter part of the walk looked as if it would be horrendously wet in normal conditions but, with everything frozen solid, my feet were still bone dry when I reached the pass and remained so all the way back to Troutbeck. Having now climbed all those fells that I could access only from south of the Kirkstone Pass, I drove back to base camp knowing that I no longer needed to worry about wintry conditions in that part of the Lake District.

Next day was, if anything, even colder, with the temperature well below freezing, but rain was forecast by early afternoon, which could make for a lot of ice. In view of this I decided to do the round from Robinson to Catbells, since I was familiar with it and with the various options it offered for getting off the fells if conditions underfoot turned nasty.

I set off early from below Catbells and made my way via Little Town to Robinson. It occurred to me on the way that I might have done better to reverse my route and at least get Catbells, Maiden Moor and High Spy under my belt before the rain arrived, since they were instantly accessible from my starting-point. However, by then the die was cast and I stuck to my original plan.

The climb up High Snab Bank to get a foothold on Robinson was every bit as steep as I remembered it and had me blowing hard in no time at all. Thankfully it is followed by an easy section which may lull the uninitiated into a false sense of security, for in no time at all one is confronted by Blea Crags and must negotiate a series of rock steps. I had thought that I would take these in my stride after my experience on Yewbarrow, but they proved to be at the limit of what I could manage: had they been icy I would have had to turn back. As it was, I just about hauled myself up them, whereafter the rest of the climb was simple, though it was a lot further to the summit cairn than I remembered.

By now the weather was deteriorating rapidly, with a bitter north-westerly blowing and Dale Head, my next objective but one, entirely concealed by cloud. It was too cold to linger on the summit and I was anxious to make as much progress as I could before the weather turned really nasty, so I hurried on to Hindscarth and from there to Dale Head. By the time I reached the latter, the cloud had lifted a little, but only to be replaced by flurries of snow which whipped past me horizontally.

Then came that part of the route I was most concerned about - the long rock staircase down to Dalehead Tarn. If that was icy, the descent would be very difficult indeed. As it turned out, I encountered no ice at all till I was almost at the foot of the staircase, whereafter there was ice in abundance, but on gentler gradients where it could be more easily sidestepped.

Having reached the tarn without incident I made my ascent of High Spy under the partial shelter of my umbrella, for by now it was raining hard. By the time I reached the top I was soaked from the waist down but, with my umbrella still up and propelled by a following wind, I hurried onwards to Blea Crag in the mistaken belief that its cairn marks the highest point of Maiden Moor. On realizing my mistake, I had to furl my umbrella and battle into a head wind and lashing rain in order to rejoin my path. I was soaked from head to foot long before I located the little pile of stones on what is indeed the highest point of Maiden Moor.

I carried on to Catbells and from there took an oblique path down to Skelgill as this represented a short-cut to the car. I was half-way down before it occurred to me that perhaps I had turned off the Catbells ridge too soon and so left the summit unclimbed, but by then I was too far down and too wet and tired to care. I reached the car acutely conscious of the fact that I had had no lunch and drove straight back to base, where I dried out and ate ravenously. Poring over my maps subsequently, I was able to establish that a) I had indeed climbed the summit of Catbells and b) I had certainly not lingered, having covered thirteen miles in just over five hours, climbing three thousand eight hundred feet (1,040 metres) in the process. I was entitled to feel tired.

Next day brought a new problem. According to the weather forecast there were police warnings of black ice on roads throughout Cumbria. Since all my remaining routes involved driving on minor roads in order to reach the starting-point, all I could come up with was to drive along the A66 to Keswick and to take the bus (if it was still running) from there to Seatoller, from where I could tackle Grey Knotts and Brandreth. However, once I was out and about the roads did not seem too bad, so I modified my plan and drove myself to the village of Grange. This may seem an odd starting-point for the two fells in question, but I did not want to risk driving up to Honister Hause.

My excessively cautious approach paid off, for just outside Grange I got a good view of a red squirrel, but it also proved unnecessary, for I reached Honister Hause without encountering any ice whatever and found the car-park at the slate-mine to be quite busy. I dithered over which route to take up Grey Knotts, opting first for the oblique route via Drum House, then changing my mind and tackling the direct ascent that follows the fence from the slate-mine all the way to the summit.

I was hoping I would not encounter any ice-covered rocks on the way, for the scope for deviating from the path appeared to be minimal. First came a long rock staircase, the steps of which were greasy enough to make me glad I was not coming down them. Having climbed that, I felt sure I must be near the summit. After all, before starting on the staircase I had already climbed up to Honister Hause, which was eleven hundred feet (335 metres) above sea level, so surely, I reasoned, it couldn't be far to go. One would have thought that by now I would have learned from experience that what you can see from the bottom, or even from halfway up, is rarely the top, but evidently I have an ingrained streak of optimism in me. In point of fact I was a lot less than halfway up and it would be a long, hard climb, altogether tougher than I expected, before I finally reached the top.

Once there, I found Grey Knotts a confusing place with various rocky spurs which might be the summit. Never having been there before I did not know which one to make for and the situation was further complicated by the fact that mist kept blowing in, obscuring first one candidate then another. By a process of trial and error I tracked down and visited both of the main contenders, then rejoined the fence which would lead me to Brandreth, completely invisible though only half a mile distant.

By the time I reached this final objective for the day, the mist had lifted enough to afford me glimpses of the formidable bulk of Great Gable, which would have to wait for another occasion. For now, I made an easy descent via Drum House to Honister Hause and so back to Grange, reaching the car as the light began to fade, for it was almost the shortest day of the year. Then it was back home with a further twelve fells in the bag, bringing my grand total to one hundred and eighty-seven. Twenty-seven to go.

Chapter Sixteen

January

WHEN I RETURNED to the Lake District towards the end of January I was wondering how I would cope after a particularly lethargic month during which the Christmas festivities had taken their toll, witness the fact that I had visited the gym just once. I had been waiting in vain for a clear spell of weather and, when that failed to materialise, I had eventually decided to come across anyway. On my first day, the forecast predicted low cloud and blustery showers, with the wind due to be strong to gale force on the fell-tops. I could well believe it, given how hard the wind was blowing down at base camp. So what was I to do? As all the ridge routes I had still to walk would take me up to at least two and a half thousand feet (760 metres), I decided to forget about them and drive to Grasmere, in the hope that I could pick off some or all of the three odd-man-out fells in the vicinity.

I started with Stone Arthur, a modest fell which I had never climbed before. The path starts alongside Greenhead Gill, from where a heron took off laboriously, startled by my approach. It had evidently not heard me coming, for the gill was rushing down towards Grasmere, all white froth after heavy overnight rain. Indeed, as I soon discovered, every little stream was full and the paths had become watercourses. My path seemed excessively steep right from the start, but perhaps that was more to do with the fact that this was my first outing since Christmas. At all events, I was soon struggling.

Doing the Wainwrights

As I climbed, minuscule patches of fresh snow became more frequent and up ahead I could see that the tops of the higher fells were dusted white. Without realizing it I by-passed Stone Arthur, the path I was on leading me towards Great Rigg on the Fairfield horseshoe. Dutifully visiting any projecting crags I passed in the belief that they might be the summit I was seeking, it was only when I looked round from one of these prominent points that I saw the summit of Stone Arthur some distance behind me. I made my way back to it and took a quick photograph of the view. Even at this modest height the wind was close to gale force and, with rain threatening, I abandoned all thoughts of continuing over Fairfield in order to get at Seat Sandal. Instead I made a swift descent to Grasmere.

After a coffee-break in the car I set off south this time for Loughrigg Fell. While still in Grasmere village I saw five deer, presumably wild, grazing in a field not a quarter of a mile from the main road. This unexpected treat put an extra spring in my step as I made my way through Deerbolts Wood to Loughrigg Terrace. I was glad to be sheltered from the wind, for it was now raining heavily, but I was not looking forward to the climb up Loughrigg Fell, which would be wholly exposed to the elements.

Luckily, the rain petered out as I emerged from the wood and it returned only sporadically thereafter, so that those occasions on which I felt obliged to risk putting up my umbrella were few and far between. On reaching the top with my umbrella safely furled, I found that the wind was gusting so strongly that I had to hang on to the elegantly constructed cairn for a moment or two to avoid being blown off my feet.

A quick descent eastwards took me out of the wind and eventually I joined the path above Rydal Water, returning to Grasmere by the delightful minor road which leads down to Dove Cottage. It was still only 2.30pm, but the rain was more or less continuous and the wind had not eased so I decided to return to base, leaving Seat Sandal for another day. I had added only two fells to my total, but a second Wainwright volume, the Central Fells, was now finished.

After blowing all night the wind finally dropped and the forecast was good, so I drove over to Crummock Water. I had five fells in my sights, the first of which was Grasmoor, which I planned to climb by way of Lad Hows. It would be a real climb, I knew, for it involves almost two and a half thousand feet (760 metres) of ascent in just one and three-quarter miles.

Setting off from Cinderdale Common, my first problem was how to cross Cinderdale Beck, which was in spate, without getting my feet soaked in the first five minutes. It took me three attempts before I found a spot where I could jump across. Then came the climb up to Lad Hows, which was certainly steep and had me shedding my down-filled jacket early on. However, it was as nothing compared to the climb that followed up Grasmoor itself. I puffed and panted my way up, shedding more layers en route and taking frequent pauses to admire the views, particularly over Crummock Water which was like a mirror, offering a perfect reflection of Mellbreak. Mist swirled around sporadically above and below me though I was never actually in it, at least until I reached the summit of Grasmoor after eighty-five minutes of unremitting effort, only to find that there was no view to be had. It was a disappointment, but at least the major part of the day's climbing was behind me now. By way of compensation, the mist soon cleared as I made for Eel Crag, which offered me splendid views north-east towards Skiddaw and south to the Scafell range.

From Eel Crag it was no more than a stroll to Wandope and from there to the lovely ridge leading up to Whiteless Pike. My first impression of this ridge had been that it looked rather too narrow and precipitous for my liking, but it turned out to be a simple, safe and enjoyable climb. I stopped for lunch on the top, from where I had an excellent view of the path I had toiled up to reach Grasmoor. It looked every bit as steep as it had felt.

Doing the Wainwrights

While lunching, I was joined by another fell-walker who told me, in a quite matter-of-fact way, that he planned to climb ten fells that day and that this was a standard target for him. Prior to that, I had thought my target of five fells quite an ambitious one, but there is always someone out there whose achievements put your own puny efforts into perspective.

I finished my lunch with a hopeful raven circling overhead, then set about the descent towards Buttermere. I half-expected it to be fearsomely steep, but it was a joy to walk, particularly in the lower reaches as it meandered towards the ridge leading to my final destination, Rannerdale Knotts.

The gentle climb on a grassy path to this last summit was again sheer delight, with excellent views all the way: south-east to Buttermere and the fells beyond, north-east to Whiteless Pike, Lad Hows and Grasmoor and, eventually and gloriously, straight ahead over Crummock Water. With the car not a stone's throw off now, the only question was how would I get down to it? I had two options. One was to go all the way back to the Whiteless Pike path and from there make my way to Crummock Water along the eastern side of Rannerdale Knotts. The other was to try and find a direct descent from the craggy summit. Wainwright records such a route and eventually I discovered it. It was extremely steep, though there is a short rock staircase for the very steepest part, which is as well since the alternative would be a scramble over loose rock and stones on what looks like a near-vertical slope. Even so, the staircase was very wet and required great care, particularly from this wimp. So painstakingly slow was my progress that it was difficult to take the honking of the numerous geese on Crummock Water as anything other than an expression of their scorn.

Eventually, and to the great relief of my thigh-muscles, I reached the road and was soon back at the car. It really had been an excellent day in near perfect conditions - no rain, no wind, no ice, relatively little cloud - and I felt privileged to have been out and about in such beautiful surroundings. I had particularly enjoyed discovering Whiteless Pike and Rannerdale Knotts and had the added satisfaction that I had now climbed all the fells in Wainwright's North-Western volume.

Next day the forecast was again good, so I decided to tackle the one outstanding route that could prove really testing, namely Great Gable and Kirk Fell by way of Base Brown and Green Gable. I set off from Seathwaite knowing that, if all went well, by the end of the day I would have completed Wainwright's Western Fells.

There was not much scope for a warm-up, as the path alongside Sour Milk Gill climbs steeply out of Seathwaite right from the start. However, it seemed to me less taxing than yesterday's climb up Grasmoor, perhaps because the rock staircase beside the gill was greasy, so that my progress was at most steady.

At the top of the staircase I opted for Wainwright's direct route up Base Brown, passing immediately beneath the dramatic Hanging Stone. From there, I had to make my way round the foot of the crags and then scramble up to a point above them, and this I found a tad scary. Did I really come up here once with Kate, our younger daughter, when she was about ten? To be fair that excursion was on a fine summer's day, with no danger of one's feet slipping but, even so, I have obviously become a lot more wimpish since then. Anyway, I psyched myself up and managed to scramble over the rocks till I was above the crags, whereafter the route to the summit was straightforward.

Ahead of me lay Green Gable, though only the bottom half of it was visible, the rest being obscured by thick cloud which blanketed the entire area. Fortunately the path is unmistakable, which was just as well since visibility was down to about fifteen metres by the time I reached the summit. Now I was within half a mile of the top of Great Gable. All I had to do was descend to Windy Gap and make the hundred and fifty metre climb up the other side. Except that, standing on top of Green Gable, I could see nothing whatever ahead of me - no Windy Gap, no Great Gable, nothing but impenetrable mist. The thought of trying to climb Great Gable - or for that matter Kirk Fell, which I had never set foot on before - in those conditions was distinctly unappealing. I turned back, reluctantly it must be said, and with many a glance over my shoulder in search of a break in the cloud, but there was none.

Somewhat crestfallen, I made my way back to Seathwaite, by-passing Base Brown this time. I was two-thirds of the way down Sour Milk Gill, with waterfalls on my left and extremely inhospitable ground on my right, when I met a young man climbing the rock staircase towards me. "Is this the way up?" he asked, as if there were a plethora of routes to choose from. I was so taken aback by his question that all I could say was "Yes". I wonder what he would have done had I said "No".

I returned to base, my hopes of completing the western fells on this occasion now dashed. It was becoming clear that it had been a mistake to leave Great Gable till so late in the scheme of things. I think the reason I had passed it over was that I regarded it as easy of access, which it is, whether via Seathwaite or Honister, but, as this outing had shown, ease of access is not everything.

I was tempted to have a second go at Great Gable next day, till I heard the forecast. With low cloud predicted all day there seemed little point, so I drove to Brothers Water instead, since from there I had a choice of two ridge routes and a one-off fell. I arrived to find everything above fifteen hundred feet (450 metres) in thick cloud.

The only strategy I could come up with was to explore the path up Caiston Glen, in the hope that the cloud might lift in the meantime and so allow me to get at some of the tops, with all of which I was unfamiliar. It soon became clear that, with one exception, the fells were almost entirely shrouded in cloud and so, abandoning Caiston Glen, I settled for climbing the exception, High Hartsop Dodd. It was a straightforward climb but, when I reached the top, marked nowadays by a small pile of stones, I found that the cloud ahead of me was as thick as ever, entirely concealing Little Hart Crag. Clearly the ridge route which would have taken me over that and on to Red Screes was out of the question and so I retraced my steps to Brothers Water.

After lunch in the car, I climbed Hartsop above How, surely a contender for the least satisfactory of all Wainwright's fells, as it is no more than one of several bumps on the long descent from Hart Crag to Deepdale Bridge. Still, it had to be climbed, so climb it I did. There was never any danger of losing the well-worn path, even in the increasingly thick mist, but it seemed a very long time before I finally reached the summit (if one can use that word of this fell). It is perhaps appropriate that there is no cairn, this distinction being reserved for what is clearly a lower point a few hundred metres away and which for some incomprehensible reason is the generally accepted summit of this non-fell.

By now the air, full of moisture, was bitterly cold and wherever tufts of grass or even single blades caught the wind they were white with an accumulation of ice. I returned by the way I had come, this being an odd-man-out fell with only one route up or down it. Back at Brothers Water, I could see that the cloud-base had not shifted all day, so I felt I had made the best of a bad job.

It was time to head home, with one hundred and ninety-eight fells climbed and just sixteen left to go. That does not sound much but, as this stay had shown, ticking off the fells in the winter months is no easy business, witness the fact that on three occasions out of four I had managed just two fells in a day. Getting the right conditions to tackle the remaining fells was clearly going to be crucial, especially where Great Gable and

Doing the Wainwrights

Kirk Fell were concerned, but how many days in the next two months were likely to be clear of both low cloud and ice? Time alone would tell.

Chapter Seventeen

The Final Fells

WELL, THIS IS IT! In early February, after what seems like weeks of low cloud, there is a three-day window of opportunity when the weather forecast is favourable and I am on my way to the Lakes to have another shot at Great Gable. As I drive across from Northumberland, the entire country seems bathed in glorious sunshine - until the Lake District comes into view, that is, and lo and behold, I see vast swathes of heavy cloud firmly ensconced on the majority of the fells. Will Great Gable and Kirk Fell be clear? I wouldn't bet on it.

As I drive through Borrowdale and up to Honister Hause, the sun disappears and the cloud becomes thicker and darker. With the prospects getting worse by the minute, all I can do is set off and hope. I know that starting from Honister Hause is a wimp's way up Great Gable, but given that not long ago I had climbed out of Seathwaite all the way to the top of Green Gable only to be baulked by low cloud I don't feel too bad about sparing myself the first thousand feet or so of the climb on this occasion. Besides, I do not have much time at my disposal for it is after midday before I set off.

It is a long haul from Honister Hause before Great Gable comes into view and, as I climb up the old tramway to Drum House and then skirt Grey Knotts and Brandreth, I wonder how much of it will be clear. When finally I get sight of it, I am delighted to find that I can see all the way to the top. But perhaps delighted is the wrong word, for the fact of the matter is that it looks terrifying, all black forbidding rock with the topmost part covered in a greyish coating which from a distance looks rather like hoar-frost and which on closer acquaintance turns out to be a mass of ice-crystals. Am I really going to get myself up there?

Well, I have to try, so I follow the path into Stone Cove, attempting as I go not to think too much about the icy rocks above. The climb up to Windy Gap is over scree, but it is not nearly as slithery as I remember it from many years ago and soon I am poised to tackle the slabs of rock that mark the real ascent to the summit. The path is steep and involves some scrambling but, so long as I do not think about what it might be like to come back down by this route, I find that I can cope remarkably well. I am soon in amongst the ice crystals I had seen from a distance, but it is only in the final hundred metres or so that they are sufficiently numerous to pose any sort of hazard.

On reaching the rock summit, I find that it is entirely covered by a film of ice and for once I forego my ritual of touching the highest point. Moving very gingerly, I manage to reach a spot where my head and shoulders are level with the highest rock, though it remains just out of reach, and I settle for that. This is eminently not the place to risk an accident - I seem to have the mountain entirely to myself - so very cautiously I retreat a few metres to a point where I can stand without risk of losing my footing and there I consult Wainwright.

I know that there is a route down the north-west ridge of Gable which leads directly to Kirk Fell, my next objective. It is the obvious route for me to take but I had decided against it before starting out, partly because I had never set foot on it before but mostly because of what Wainwright has to say about it. He talks of "shifting scree" and describes the ridge as "relentlessly rough and steep", which did not sound like my cup of tea at all. But now that I am here on top of Gable I am

Route 42b. Yewbarrow from Middle Fell, with the head
of Wast Water and the two giants, Scafell Pike
and (right of picture) Scafell.

Route 42b. The breathtaking Wasdale Screes
seen from Buckbarrow.

Route 45. Grasmere and Rydal Water from Silver How
on a perfectly still October morning.

Route 45. Easedale Tarn from near Blea Rigg
on a day when low cloud enhanced the landscape.

Route 46. The second and third Crinkles, seen from the first. The Bad Step, a large slab of rock two-thirds of the way down the second Crinkle, is clearly visible. My path veers away from it to the left.

Route 47. "How on earth do I get up that?" The seemingly inaccessible Harrison Stickle viewed from Pike How.

Route 47. The uppermost section of Pike o'Stickle.
I really wasn't sure I could cope with this.

Route 47. The Langdale Pikes seen in all their glory
from near Side Pike.

Route 49. Carrock Fell from the west
on a bitterly cold November day.

Route 51. A fine view south-west from near Boardale Hause
to Arnison Crag, with Birks and Saint Sunday Crag beyond.

Route 51. Angle Tarn looking summery in November.

Route 51. In fact, much of it was iced over.

Route 52. The entire Helvellyn range, from Great Dodd southwards, seen from the summit of Causey Pike. In the centre of the picture, the tip of Catbells projects (just) above the clouds.

Route 52. South-west from Sail. The central ridge is Maiden Moor and High Spy.

Route 52. Causey Pike seen from Sail. In the distance, Blencathra on the left and the Dodds on the right.

Base Camp.

Route 53. The main summit cairn on Ill Bell,
where I enjoyed a sunny December picnic.

Route 57. Crummock Water and Loweswater from the Lad
How path. Believe it or not, but it's January!

Route 57. Grasmoor from Whiteless Pike.
My route up (and up and up!) follows the central curve.

Route 58. The Hanging Stone on Base Brown.
One does not linger hereabouts.

Route 60. The ice-covered summit of Great Gable.

Route 61. Caiston Beck almost entirely turned to ice.

Route 61. High Hartsop Dodd (centre foreground)
and Brothers Water from Little Hart Crag.

Route 62. On the summit of Rampsgill Head,
the first of nine fells on a perfect February day.

Route 62. The head of Ullswater seen from Hartsop Dodd.

Route 64.
"We're heading up there!" On the slopes of Blencathra in March.

Celebrating on top of
Blencathra.

Celebrating at home. In front of the cake is Jen's model of
me on Blencathra summit. On the map to the right,
214 red dots show that the job is done.

Summit cairns come in all shapes and sizes

GRISEDALE PIKE

CLOUGH HEAD

STARLING DODD

COLD PIKE

GRIKE

BLACK FELL

HART SIDE

BLEABERRY FELL

beginning to have second thoughts. Why? Because the only alternative is to return to Stone Cove by the way I have just come - in itself a tall order - and then find the north traverse round the head of Great Gable to that point from which I can climb Kirk Fell. Can I risk such a huge detour when I have so little time at my disposal?

After re-reading what Wainwright has to say about the north-west ridge and reminding myself of the ice that I would doubtless have to negotiate on that route, it doesn't take me long to decide. I will go down the way I came up - that at least is a known quantity - and if in the process I run out of time to tackle Kirk Fell, so be it.

Wimp that I am, I make my way back to Stone Cove, coping with the downward scramble better than I would have thought - perhaps because the only alternative seems so much worse. The path below the north face of Great Gable proves easy to follow and soon I am making the ascent of Kirk Fell, which seems simple by comparison with what has gone before. When I get the opportunity I look back at the north-west ridge of Gable and am appalled by what I see. It is long, very steep, with a lot of scree and parts of it are covered in sheets of ice. Thank heavens I'm a wimp!

After a quick exploration of the summit of Kirk Fell, I return to Stone Cove and from there to Honister Hause, reaching the car with the light fading fast. I am tired and hungry - there has been no time to stop and eat - but above all I feel hugely relieved that at last I have Gable behind me. By comparison, the fourteen fells that remain to be climbed are all straightforward, or so I imagine in my euphoria. And I have now climbed all of Wainwright's Western Fells.

I wake next morning to a bright but bitterly cold day - the temperature on the fell-tops is forecast to be minus four celsius - and drive to Brothers Water with thoughts of climbing five fells, three to the west of the Kirkstone Pass and two to the east.

Doing the Wainwrights

I start on the western side, walking up to Scandale Pass by way of Caiston Beck. The stream is more ice than water and there is plenty of ice on the path as well. From the top of the pass Little Hart Crag, my first objective, comes into view, looking delightful in the sunshine. I thoroughly enjoy the simple climb to the summit, which I explore briskly for there is a strong and bitterly cold wind blowing. Then I return to the Scandale Pass and go straight up the other side to the summit of Red Screes. From here the views are outstanding but there is no sign of the path which, according to Wainwright, drops down to the head of the Kirkstone Pass. Perhaps this is not surprising, for the ground falls away so sharply on the eastern side that, from the summit, any path could easily be concealed from view. Besides, I have already decided that whether there is a path or not is a matter of academic interest, for I have seen enough to convince me that there is no way down from here that I can cope with.

Instead I follow the ridge north to Middle Dodd, my third objective for the day and the last on the western side of the Kirkstone Pass. On my way I keep an eye open for another route recorded by Wainwright which links this ridge with the Kirkstone Pass, but the ground here is, if anything, even steeper than at the summit and I abandon all thoughts of doing any climbing to the east of the pass.

The descent from Middle Dodd to Caiston Beck is quite gentle by comparison with the routes I have been considering but it is amply steep enough for my taste, and by the time I get back to Brothers Water my legs are more than ready to call it a day. I feel a bit uncomfortable about doing so when it is only 3pm and the weather is still excellent, but in the circumstances there seems no alternative. I drive back to base knowing that I have eleven fells still to climb and that there is the prospect of one more day of good weather ahead of me.

Next day turns out to be the sort of day fell-walkers dream about, with clear skies and perfect visibility. Moreover, the wind has dropped so that, although it remains very cold, it no longer feels so bitter. As I drive over to Hartsop, near Brothers Water, I encounter a fox in the middle of the road, uncertain which way to go. Eventually, after a little dance on the tarmac, he dives off into the undergrowth and I drive on, delighted to have been entertained in this way.

From Hartsop I take the track up beside Hayeswater Gill. Once again there is a lot of ice in evidence and one of the tributaries of the gill is frozen solid all the way down a steep rock-face. In the gill itself a pair of dippers are acting out their courtship ritual, the male displaying by flapping his little wings furiously. It is good to be reminded that, despite all the ice, spring is in the air.

On reaching Hayeswater, which is almost entirely frozen over, I climb up beside The Knott and cut across to Rampsgill Head, my first fell of the day. The cairn marking the summit is more prominent than it was in Wainwright's day and the views in all directions are simply breath-taking. I can see so many summits that it is as if the entire Lake District were visible from this one spot.

I am joined by a jogger doing a recce for the Joss Naylor Challenge, of which I have never heard. Apparently it is restricted to over-fifties and involves getting from Pooley Bridge in the east to Wasdale in the west within twelve hours, taking in a great many fells en route, including Bowfell, Great Gable and Pillar. The magnitude of the challenge is evident, but my companion seems quite undaunted by it and trots off westwards heading for High Street, while I, humbled by what I have heard, head east for High Raise.

It is an easy walk on a gently rising, grass-covered slope and I bowl along, tingling with excitement in the knowledge that any moment now the number of fells left to climb will be down to single figures. No sooner am I on the summit of High Raise than I turn my attention to my next target, Kidsty Pike, which is likewise near at hand and easy of access. Fifteen minutes later I am standing on top of my third fell of the day. Next comes a longer but still easy stretch over grassland to High Street, where I pause for lunch before heading off south-east to my fifth fell, Mardale Ill Bell. That too is an easy walk and from there a good path takes me north-west to Thornthwaite Crag, by which point I have six fells under my belt and it is still only 1.30pm!

The sunshine is surprisingly warm as I walk from Thornthwaite Crag over the long, grassy ridge of Gray Crag to its summit cairn, which lies at the northernmost tip of the fell. From here my plan is to descend to Hayeswater and so back to the car. However, I am feeling so elated by the progress I have made and there are still so many hours of daylight left that I decide to try and add to the day's tally by tackling the two fells east of the Kirkstone Pass which had eluded me yesterday. I turn about and make my way back towards Thornthwaite Crag before swinging west to Threshthwaite Mouth.

Here I face my first serious challenge of the day, for rising ahead of me is a barrier of rock, glistening with patches of ice and festooned with icicles, which bars the way to my next destination, Stony Cove Pike. Somehow or other I have to get myself over these rocks, which I have never climbed before. Uncomfortably aware of Wainwright's warning that this route could be dangerous in icy conditions, I start to climb and almost immediately am confronted by a huge slab of rock. Eventually I manage to lever myself over it and, after that initial challenge, the ascent proves much less difficult than it had looked. The patches of ice I encounter are easily by-passed and there is only one more slightly awkward scramble to be made. Soon I am on the top of Caudale Moor, where I locate the summit, Stony Cove Pike, before making the long descent to my ninth and final fell of the day, Hartsop Dodd.

I have now outstripped my record for one day - the eight fells of the Fairfield horseshoe - and have just two fells left to climb in the entire Lake District. All of this is a cause for celebration, but I have still to get off Hartsop Dodd. Reaching its summit has involved almost no effort at all, the way from Stony Cove Pike being almost wholly downhill, but getting off it is an entirely different matter. Wainwright records three routes but, since my destination is Hartsop, only the direct descent by the north ridge makes any sense and what a descent that proves to be! At times the ground falls away so sharply beneath me that the only way I can avoid an onset of vertigo is by focusing fiercely on the path immediately ahead of me as it twists and turns, sticking always to the line of the ridge and dropping steeply all the way to Hartsop. Fortunately the ground is bone hard with most of the loose stones that litter the path frozen together, making ideal conditions for tackling this descent. If the stones were loose and the grass damp, it would be more like a ski-run.

I reach Hartsop six and a quarter hours after setting out and the sun is still shining. It has been a truly memorable day, not least because I had fully expected the nine fells I have climbed to keep me occupied for two full days. Now just two fells are left - Seat Sandal and Blencathra. What, I wonder, will tomorrow bring?

It brings a distinct change in the weather, with the cloud-base down to about fifteen hundred feet (450 metres) and the air bitterly cold, much colder than yesterday. The plan for the day is simple: to climb Seat Sandal, which I have never visited before. The question is, how to go about it? One option is to drive to the top of Dunmail Raise and start from there, in the process saving five hundred feet (150 metres) of ascent and halving the overall distance as compared with a start from Grasmere. I consider the possibility but dismiss it because it seems like cheating, particularly as I will be climbing just this one fell today, so I drive down to Grasmere and start from there.

The climb proper gets under way when I reach the foot of

Great Tongue. I take the path on its western side, which turns out to be extremely steep, making for slow progress. Once on the top of Great Tongue I get in amongst the ice and my progress slows still more. The path leading me to Grisedale Hause is a high-level one and several times I am forced to abandon it when it disappears beneath large sheets of ice. In fact I find this whole section of the route, for all its modest altitude, scarcely less testing than the top of Great Gable.

On reaching Grisedale Hause, I turn west for the final, steep ascent of Seat Sandal and soon find myself in thick mist with visibility down to about five metres. On a good many fells this would be a serious problem, but here the path follows a wall to within thirty metres of the summit, so that even I cannot go wrong. Even so, with no other fell-walkers in evidence, it feels very isolated as I climb up to the point at which I have to leave the wall and track down the summit-cairn. The latter is quite invisible from the wall itself, but, counting my paces, I come to it in precisely thirty steps, as Wainwright had informed me that I would. I touch it and promptly return to the relative shelter of the wall, to escape the bitter wind.

The descent to Grisedale Hause requires care, but I manage it without incident and am greatly relieved when at last I emerge from the mist and can see other fell-walkers on the main path down to Grasmere. There are even a couple of fell-runners in action, though how they manage to keep their feet with so much ice about I have no idea.

This time I take the path on the eastern side of Great Tongue and, though it has its fair share of ice, I find it altogether easier than my outward route. Still, by the time I am back at Grasmere I know that I have been on a testing excursion.

Now all that remains is Blencathra - that at least has worked out according to plan. I drive home feeling confident that, with seven weeks in hand, I will indeed complete the task within the allotted twelve months.

The Final Fells

16 March 2006. Nearly five weeks have elapsed since I was last in the Lake District, three of them taken up by a complete rewire of our house plus the aftermath, the remaining two spent waiting for some fine weather. The plan was for Jen and me to go across to the Lakes together: I would climb Blencathra, we would celebrate and then have a couple of days doing wheelchair walks in the spring sunshine. Unfortunately, as at the beginning of this whole venture, the weather has had other ideas. The country generally and the Lake District in particular have remained firmly in the grip of winter and in the end, with time beginning to run out and with no prospect of a change in the weather, I have come across on my own for the final climb.

Except that this time I will not be on my own. Two friends from our village who have followed the progress of this madcap undertaking from its beginnings are coming across to join me on the climb up Blencathra. We are due to meet at the White Horse Inn, immediately below Scales Fell. As I set off from base camp for the rendezvous, the prospects are not exactly bright, for it is snowing hard and there is a bitterly cold north-east wind. At least the snow is not settling down here in the valley, but I find myself wondering what the fell-top has in store for us. According to the forecast, the temperature on the tops is likely to be minus four celsius, with a high wind-chill factor making it feel more like minus fourteen - not the best place for a party.

I arrive at the White Horse Inn to find it 'closed for essential repairs', so bang go any thoughts of a last-minute warm-up before we set off or a thaw-out and a celebratory drink when we finish. I just hope the climb won't prove to be another non-event. Fortunately, my friends have come prepared for mid-winter and we set off, muffled up to the eyebrows and looking like three characters out of Nanouk of the North.

I have known, from even before I set foot on Binsey almost a year ago, what the route would be up this final fell. In my head I think of it as 'the angina route'. It is the one I took on that summer's day in 2002 when angina first erupted into my life: up to the top by Doddick Fell and down by Scales Fell and Mousthwaite Comb. My companions are happy to humour me in this respect and we make our way to Scaley Beck, cross it and scramble up the other side onto Doddick Fell.

By now the snow showers have stopped and we even get spells of sunshine, during which we can see clearly all the way to the top. Today Blencathra is divided into two parts: the bottom third dark with vegetation, the top two-thirds progressively more white. Soon there is a sprinkling of snow underfoot and then, increasingly, patches of ice. By the time we reach the rock turrets at the top of Doddick Fell, the snow and ice have become continuous and, suddenly, keeping our footing is no easy matter. A path by-passes the rock turrets on the right and, being a wimp, I take it as I always have done. Today, however, it proves anything but an easy option and I am glad when we reach the main ridge which will take us up to the summit of Blencathra.

From here the path ascends in a series of zig-zags and the further we advance the more slippery it becomes. Given that none of us has crampons, it is tempting to abandon the path for the hummocks of grass, but these too are iced over and prove even more difficult to walk on. We settle for the path and progress slowly, keeping where possible to the loose snow, though frequently that is no more than a thin layer covering the ice beneath. Indeed one of my companions hits the deck, cheerfully, at least three times before we are back on terra firma.

Eventually we make it to the top where, incomprehensibly, we are spared the worst of the wind and can celebrate with photographs, chocolate and Schnapps (on which I pass). I ring Jen from the summit to share the excitement. I feel really elated to be up here, but at the same time I know that the job is not yet done. The ice is going to be much more difficult on the way down and the weather is not getting any better.

The Final Fells

In fact it starts snowing again while we are on the top and visibility is down to about fifteen metres as we leave the summit. Now we are walking straight into a head wind and it starts to feel bitterly cold, not least because, with all the ice underfoot, we can only advance at a snail's pace. Progress remains slow till we reach Scales Fell, at which point the ice gradually disappears and we are able to stride out once more. In Mousthwaite Comb we at last find shelter from the wind and take a much-delayed lunch-break. We also find the first frog-spawn I have seen this year, which is somehow fitting, for it feels very much as if we have left winter up on the fell behind us.

We return to the White Horse Inn three hours and fifty-five minutes after setting off, which for a route of just over four miles is an all-time slow. This is in large measure due to the conditions, which without doubt have been worse than anything I have encountered throughout my year on the fells, so it has been a good route to do in company.

My overriding feeling on reaching the road is one of relief. Relief that we have managed to get off Blencathra safely and relief that I have managed the last of the Wainwrights before time ran out on me. We head back to base camp and celebrate with mulled wine. The challenge is over with just a fortnight to spare.

Conclusion

DOING THE WAINWRIGHTS is not, I fancy, something of which Wainwright himself would have approved. To a man who so clearly revelled in the detailed exploration of each fell, who meticulously plotted every route up and down, who above all took ample time to savour the experience, preferably in solitude, the idea of a steadily growing horde of fell-walkers dashing from one fell to the next in order to tick off those that are on the list while ignoring those that are not must surely be anathema. For doing the Wainwrights is a popular activity these days, witness the paths that have been beaten to the most unprepossessing fell-tops - provided that they feature in Wainwright's volumes - and above all the neat little cairn that has been erected to mark that most elusive of spots, the highest point of Mungrisdale Common.

I have to admit that over the last twelve months I have tended to hurry from one fell to the next and that the freedom to explore and enjoy to the full the delights of any particular fell has been in short supply. But on the other hand, doing the Wainwrights has taken me to parts of the Lake District which almost certainly I would never have visited otherwise. It has been a journey of discovery for, of the two hundred and fourteen fells in question, one hundred and nine were entirely new to me, while many others I had visited so long ago as to have almost no recollection of them. As a result, I now have a long list of fells I want to revisit and to explore in a more leisurely fashion, and perhaps in that way I can make my peace with Wainwright's shade.

As well as having a lot to look forward to, I have a lot of

Conclusion

memories from the past twelve months, most of which this book has recorded. If I had to pick out the best expedition of all, it would be the day in May when I climbed Steeple, Pillar and company, though at least three other excursions - the Coniston Fells in July, the Langdale Pikes and Lingmoor Fell in October and the fells around High Street in February - would run it close. All of these occasions were blessed with exceptionally good weather and all took me, at least part of the time, into unknown territory, affording the special delight that comes from discovering a new fell under clear skies.

The most dismal outing is easy to identify, for the day I climbed Sallows, Sour Howes and Wansfell in thick mist had nothing to recommend it, whereas I at least had something to look at when I was getting soaked to the skin on Ard Crags and Knott Rigg or on Great Crag

As for the most hair-raising experience, that too is easy. The day in August when I tackled Hard Knott, Slight Side and Scafell wins by a mile, though that is almost entirely down to the business of driving over the Hardknott Pass. As for the fells themselves, Mellbreak in April and Eagle Crag in May tested me most sternly, with Yewbarrow not far behind.

But overall there has been infinitely more pleasure than pain. Indeed, in a purely physical sense pain has been entirely absent, barring the odd blister. My heart has coped with everything I have asked of it and never once, even in the bitterest conditions, have I needed to take my spray. And I have got fitter over the year, no doubt about it. I am convinced that now I could take the Fairfield horseshoe in my stride, though back in April 2005 it just about finished me off. I may even have got a little bolder too. I hesitate to say that I could now cope with Wainwright's route A up Mellbreak but, having scrambled up Yewbarrow and reached the top of an ice-bound Great Gable, I do feel that I have pushed the psychological barriers back a little, though for how long remains to be seen.

Doing the Wainwrights

As for the statistics, I find that I needed sixty-four expeditions in order to climb all two hundred and fourteen fells, making an average of exactly three and one quarter fells per outing. In the process, I walked six hundred and forty-one miles in three hundred and twenty-six and a half hours and climbed one hundred and seventy-one thousand, three hundred feet (52,212 metres). On the fund-raising front, the total amount raised was an extremely pleasing £2,228, the equivalent of just over £10.41 for every single fell.

The feeling of relief I experienced at getting the final fell under my belt has now mellowed into a sense of satisfaction. As I sit at home looking at the map of the Lake District with its mass of red dots - one for each fell climbed - it is a source of pleasure to think that, despite the haphazard nature of my planning and despite all my wimpish misgivings en route, the scheme has come to fruition. With the advantage of hindsight, I can see that it was right to get ahead of schedule during the spring and summer months and to focus on the least accessible fells. It even turns out that April was a good time to make a start, for conditions in February and March this year have proved very difficult indeed and I cannot see that I would have got anywhere near climbing twenty fells in either of those months.

Not that I can take credit for the weather. What it all really boils down to is that I have been lucky, enormously lucky. Lucky to have had the weather on my side. Lucky to have managed the whole thing without any physical setbacks. Lucky, on so many occasions, to have found myself in such beautiful places. Lucky to be alive.

Appendix

What follows is a list of the routes I took, in the order in which I took them. It should be used in conjunction with Wainwright's Pictorial Guide to the Lakeland Fells, referred to as AW. Chapter numbers refer to the relevant section of Doing the Wainwrights. Intermediate times are given in brackets and are cumulative. Total times include all stops en route for whatever purpose.

Chapter Two

1a. Binsey (Northern Fells).

O.S. Explorer OL 4. Park near Binsey Lodge (GR 236352). Follow AW's direct route to the top (15 minutes). Descend by reversing his route of ascent from High Ireby. From Ruthwaite, walk S along the road to Binsey Lodge.

3.5 miles/5.5 kms. 760ft/230m ascent. 1 hour 30.

1b. Great Cockup - Meal Fell - Great Sca Fell - Brae Fell - Longlands Fell (Northern Fells).

O.S. Explorer OL 4. Use the car-park by Over Water (GR 256354). Walk by road to Longlands bridge (GR 266358; there is limited parking here, if preferred). Take the valley path skirting the western side of Longlands Fell and Lowthwaite Fell and passing through Trusmadoor. Just beyond the cliffs of Trusmadoor, turn off right and climb steeply, skirting the cliff edge before heading W to the top of Great Cockup. Return to Trusmadoor and follow AW's ridge routes to Meal Fell, Great Sca Fell and Brae Fell (from Great Sca Fell avoid the temptation to head E of N which leads not to Brae Fell but to Yard Steel). From Brae Fell a good path describes a semi-circle SW to Lowthwaite Fell and Longlands Fell. Descend to Longlands by reversing AW's route of ascent and so back to the car.

9.5 miles/15kms. 2,165ft/660m ascent. 3 hours 40.

Appendix

2. Nab Scar - Heron Pike - Great Rigg - Fairfield - Hart Crag - Dove Crag - High Pike - Low Pike (Eastern Fells).

O.S. Explorer OL 5 and 7. Limited parking beside Rydal Church (GR365063) or in the nearby car-park just W of Pelter Bridge (GR 365059). Follow AW's route from Rydal up Nab Scar (50 minutes) and his ridge routes from there out to Fairfield (2 hours 30) and back to Low Pike. To descend to Ambleside (5 hours 50), follow his route from Low Pike by High or Low Sweden Bridge. Walk back to Rydal along the A591 (if you have the energy - I didn't - a track on your right just after Scandale Bridge takes you to the church via Rydal Park).

10.75 miles/17 kms. 3,330ft/1,015m ascent. 6 hours 35.

N.B. This is the Fairfield horseshoe, clockwise. It can of course be walked anti-clockwise, if preferred.

3. Mellbreak - Hen Comb (Western Fells).

O.S. Explorer OL 4. Limited parking just beyond Church Bridge, Loweswater (GR 142208). Take AW's route C from Loweswater to the north top of Mellbreak (1 hour 45 after attempting and abandoning route B). From there visit the marginally higher south top, then descend to Mosedale by route C and turn right. Leave the Loweswater track where the path for Hen Comb crosses Mosedale Beck (GR137199). Follow AW's route of ascent via Little Dodd and return the same way to Loweswater.

9.5 miles/15kms. 2,685ft/820m ascent. 5 hours.

4. Bowscale Fell - Bannerdale Crags - Mungrisdale Common - Souther Fell (Northern Fells).

O.S. Explorer OL 5. Start from Mungrisdale (GR 364303). Take AW's route 1 from Mungrisdale up Bowscale Fell (1 hour), then follow his ridge route to Bannerdale Crags (1 hour 25). Descend W to the Glenderamackin col (GR 327293) and continue W, climbing very gently to the cairn - not easily found - on Mungrisdale Common (2 hours 10). Return to the Glenderamackin col and descend on the north side of the River Glenderamackin to the footbridge. Cross the river and climb to the col above Mousthwaite Comb (GR 346279). Take the path NE to Souther Fell (3 hours 45): the summit is about 800 metres short of the northern tip. Return to the bridge over the River Glenderamackin and follow the riverside path downstream to Mungrisdale.

12.25 miles/19.5 kms. 2,105ft/640m ascent. 5 hours 25.

N.B. Blencathra can be easily added to this route by walking SE from the cairn on Mungrisdale Common. From the summit of Blencathra, head N and descend over Foule Crag to the Glenderamackin col.

Chapter Three

5. Selside Pike - Branstree - Tarn Crag - Grey Crag (Far Eastern Fells).

O.S. Explorer OL 5 and 7. Limited roadside parking where the Old Corpse Road leaves the Mardale Head road (GR 479118). Follow the Old Corpse Road to the ridge running SW, which leads up to Selside Pike. From there take AW's ridge routes to Branstree (1 hour 30), Tarn Crag and Grey Crag (2 hours 40). AW's route of descent from Grey Crag to Sadgill is far from obvious - I came out at Stockdale Bridge (GR 490050), about two-thirds of a mile further S (3 hours 55). Cross to Mardale Head by Gatescarth Pass (N.B. this involves 1,280ft/390m of ascent) and so back to your starting-point.

12.75 miles/20.5 kms. 3,590ft/1,095m ascent. 6 hours 30.

6. Allen Crags - Glaramara - Rosthwaite Fell (Southern Fells).

O.S. Explorer OL 4 and 6. Park at Seathwaite (GR 235123). Take AW's route up Allen Crags by way of Stockley Bridge and Ruddy Gill, eventually bearing left off the main track on a path which leads directly to Allen Crags (1 hour 45). Follow AW's ridge routes to Glaramara and Rosthwaite Fell (5 hours. N.B. The route to Bessyboot on Rosthwaite Fell is far from clear - allow plenty of time). Descend between Rottenstone Gill and Dry Gill to Combe Gill. Cross the latter and follow the path down towards the Seatoller road. Just before reaching Strands

Bridge (GR 252137), turn left along a track heading SW back to Seathwaite.

9.5 miles/15.25 km. 2,950ft/900m ascent. 6 hours 30.

7. Barf - Lord's Seat - Broom Fell - Graystones - Whinlatter (North-Western Fells).

O.S. Explorer OL 4. Limited parking beside the old A66 N of Thornthwaite (GR 224258) or in the Powter How car-park (GR 222265). From the hotel take AW's route through Beckstones Plantation to Barf (65 minutes), a very steep climb. Follow his ridge routes to Lord's Seat (1 hour 30), Broom Fell (1 hour 50) and Graystones (2 hours 30). Make a steep descent S towards Scawgill Bridge. Three-quarters of the way down (GR 177258), turn left onto a forestry path and eventually cross Aiken Beck. Walk E along the track above the beck, leaving it to climb up to Brown How (GR 192253) wherever the plantations allow. Follow the ridge SE to the summit of Whinlatter. Descend steeply ESE to Thornthwaite Forest, where a good path leads to the visitor centre and from there above Comb Beck to Thornthwaite village. Left along the road to the car.

8.5 miles/13.5 kms. 2,940ft/896m ascent. 6 hours 20.

N.B. The route between Graystones and Brown How was improvised: it is not a recognised right of way. The time reflects the difficulty of route-finding between Graystones and Whinlatter, plus a detour made necessary by the temporary closure of the path down to Thornthwaite village.

8. Arnison Crag - Birks - Saint Sunday Crag (Eastern Fells).

O.S. Explorer OL 5. Start from Patterdale. Take AW's route up Arnison Crag (45 minutes), following the wall that encloses Glemara Park. Continue SW to Trough Head (GR 388144) and from there follow AW's route up to Birks (1 hour 30) and his ridge route to Saint Sunday Crag (2 hours 25), visiting Gavel Pike en route. Descend via Deepdale Hause to Grisedale Tarn (there is a good path nowadays). Return to Patterdale by the Grisedale valley.

9 miles/14.5 kms. 2,465ft/755m ascent. 5 hours 15.

Chapter Five

9. Steeple - Scoat Fell - Pillar - Red Pike - Haycock - Caw Fell (Western Fells).

O.S. Explorer OL 4. Car-park at the foot of Bowness Knott (GR 109153). Take the track alongside Ennerdale Water to Char Dub bridge (GR 134142). Cross the River Liza and the fields beyond to the forest. Follow a track heading S which bears left and crosses Woundell Beck to join AW's route of ascent to Steeple (2 hours 45). Follow his ridge routes to Scoat Fell and Pillar (3 hours 40). Return to Scoat Fell but well before the summit bear left on a good path S then SSE to Red Pike (5 hours). Return to Scoat Fell summit and take AW's ridge route to Haycock (5 hours 55) and Caw Fell (6 hours 40). Descend to Char Dub by reversing AW's route of ascent from Ennerdale: the path through the forest is now clear and easy to follow. Take the track beside Ennerdale Water back to the car-park.

16 miles/25.5 kms. 4,070ft/1,240m ascent. 9 hours.

10. Ling Fell - Sale Fell (North-Western Fells).

O.S. Explorer OL 4. Limited parking off the Wythop Mill road near its junction with the A66 (GR 175304). Follow AW's route up Ling Fell (50 minutes). Descend NE to the track above Burthwaite and so back to your point of access to the fell (GR 183292). Turn right along the road and first left down a steep hill to Wythop Beck. At the junction turn right and follow the farm road to Kelswick. From here take AW's route up Sale Fell

(2 hours). Descend by reversing AW's route of ascent from Bassenthwaite Lake Station. At the road, turn left to Wythop Mill and so back to the car.

6.25 miles/10 kms. 1,650ft/505m ascent. 2 hours 55.

11. Eagle Crag - Sergeant's Crag - High Raise - Sergeant Man - Thunacar Knott - Ullscarf (Central Fells).

O.S. Explorer OL 4 and 6. Start from Rosthwaite (GR 257148). Cross Stonethwaite Beck and follow the path upstream to Stonethwaite. From here take AW's route A (not for the faint-hearted, who should take route B) up Eagle Crag (1 hour 55). Follow his ridge routes to Sergeant's Crag (2 hours 20), High Raise (3 hours 20), Sergeant Man (4 hours after a lunch-stop) and Thunacar Knott (4 hours 25). Return to High Raise and take AW's ridge route to Ullscarf (5 hours 55). Descend to Watendlath by reversing his route of ascent (there is a good path down as far as Low Saddle: thereafter it is guess-work) and take the track SW back to Rosthwaite.

14.75 miles/23.5 kms. 4,540ft/1,075m ascent. 8 hours.

12. Clough Head (Eastern Fells).

O.S. Explorer OL 5. Limited roadside parking at Wanthwaite Bridge (GR 315232). Walk E to the Threlkeld road and turn right. The first track on the left marks the start of AW's route up Clough Head (1 hour 20), by way of the Old Coach Road and White Pike. Continue SSW to Calfhow Pike and return to the Old Coach Road at Mariel Bridge (GR 350227) by way of

Mosedale Beck. Follow the Old Coach Road back to the Threlkeld road and so to Wanthwaite Bridge.

8 miles/13 kms. 2,020ft/615m ascent. 3 hours 35.

13. Harter Fell - Kentmere Pike - Shipman Knotts (Far Eastern Fells).

O.S. Explorer OL 7. Start from Mardale Head (GR 469108). Take AW's route from the road end by way of Nan Bield Pass to Harter Fell (1 hour 25). Follow his ridge routes to Kentmere Pike (1 hour 55) and Shipman Knotts (3 hours), visiting Goat Scar en route. Descend by the wall to the pass (GR 476049) between Stile End and Sadgill. Turn right to Stile End and the Kentmere valley road (3 hours 50). Turn right along the road, into the track past Overend (GR 464057) and up to the Nan Bield Pass (5 hours 25), leaving Tongue Scar (GR 454071) on your left as you climb. From the head of the pass, return by your outward route to Mardale Head.

10.75 miles/17 kms. 3,290ft/1,005m ascent. 6 hours 10.

14. Place Fell - Hallin Fell - Beda Fell (Far Eastern Fells).

O.S. Explorer OL 5. Start from Patterdale. Take the track to Side Farm (GR 397163). Turn right and follow the track to a gate (GR 401163). Pass through this and immediately turn left through another gate onto the open fell. Here turn right and climb up to Boardale Hause (GR 407157). Take the path N to Place Fell (1 hour 5). Head NE, passing High Dodd (GR 415183) on your left and making a very steep descent over Sleet

Fell to Sandwick (see AW's ascent of Place Fell from Sandwick). Follow the road to the church of St. Peter's (GR 435193) and climb straight up Hallin Fell (2 hours 45). Return to the church and follow the road S past Martindale old church to Wintercrag Farm (GR 434184). A path on the right heads NW and meets the path (GR 431186) which climbs over Winter Crag and up the north ridge of Beda Fell to the summit (4 hours 25). Descend over Bedafell Knott to Boardale Hause and so back to Patterdale.

10.75 miles/17 kms. 3,565ft/1,090m ascent. 5 hours 40.

15a. Castle Crag (North-Western Fells).

O.S. Explorer OL 4. Start from Grange (GR 253175). Follow AW's route of ascent (45 minutes). To descend, reverse his route of ascent from Rosthwaite, but instead of crossing the River Derwent follow it S to Longthwaite (GR 256144). Cross the river here and take the path on your left to Rosthwaite, where a track on your left leads back to the River Derwent. Cross it again and follow it downstream to Grange.

7 miles/11.5 kms. 665ft/205m ascent. 2 hours 30.

15b. Grange Fell (Central Fells).

O.S. Explorer OL 4. Start from Grange and follow AW's route of ascent by turning right after Grange Bridge and left onto the open fell and so to the top of Brund Fell (50 minutes). Cross the wall E of Jopplety How and descend S by a wall to the Rosthwaite-Watendlath path (GR 267158). Here turn right for Rosthwaite. As the descent steepens, turn right onto a path (GR 264155) through Frith Wood, joining the Borrowdale road at Red Brow (GR 256158). Return to Grange by the road.

4.5 miles/7 kms. 1,300ft/395m ascent. 1 hour 55.

N.B. These two routes were a response to bad weather. The intention had been to start from Grange, climb Grange Fell, then Great Crag (Central Fells), descend to Rosthwaite, climb Castle Crag and so back to Grange.

16. Gowbarrow Fell - Little Mell Fell (Eastern Fells).

O.S. Explorer OL 5. Limited parking at Dockray (GR 394216). Opposite the inn a track heads E. Follow this, turning right at the junction after Riddings Beck. Pass through a stone wall (GR 398215) and follow it to the top of Gowbarrow Fell (30 minutes). Descend ESE to the ruins of the shooting-box (GR 414217) and take the path running NE by Little Meldrum to the Watermillock road (GR 432233). Turn left along the road and climb up to The Hause where a permissive path leads to the summit of Little Mell Fell (1 hour 50). Return to the road and turn right then left along a minor road to Ulcat Row. Where the road makes a right-angle bend (GR 404226) continue straight ahead on a footpath which eventually rejoins your outward route, at which point turn right and so back to Dockray.

7 miles/11 kms. 1,470ft/445m ascent. 3 hours.

N.B. Great Mell Fell (route 21 below) can easily be incorporated into this route by taking the path at the foot of Little Mell Fell to Lowthwaite and turning right along the minor road to

Nabend. Here turn left and left again after the bridge and so to the starting-point for the ascent of Great Mell Fell. To return to Dockray afterwards, go by road to Ulcat Row and rejoin the route above.

Chapter Six

17. Walla Crag (Central Fells).

O.S. Explorer OL 4. Start from Keswick. Follow AW's route of ascent to the top (55 minutes). Return by the same route as far as Rakefoot (GR 284222), then follow the minor road to the A591 and return to Keswick.

5 miles/8 kms. 1,000ft/305m ascent. 2 hours 15.

N.B. Weather and time permitting, there is no reason why Bleaberry Fell and High Seat should not be climbed in conjunction with Walla Crag. See route 29 below.

18. Latrigg (Northern Fells).

O.S. Explorer OL 4. Limited parking at Briar Rigg, Keswick (GR 268242). Follow the track (Spooney Green Lane) over the A66 to the Gale Road car-park (GR 282254) and walk SSW up the path to the summit (50 minutes). Descend the eastern slope till the path joins a minor road (GR 296252) above Brundholme and follow this W through Brundholme Wood, over the A66 and so back to Briar Rigg.

5 miles/8 kms. 950ft/290m ascent. 1 hour 50.

N.B. When circumstances permit, it is a simple matter to include Latrigg when climbing Skiddaw and/or Lonscale Fell from the south. See route 40 below.

Appendix

19. Steel Knotts - Wether Hill - Loadpot Hill - Bonscale Pike - Arthur's Pike (Far Eastern Fells).

O.S. Explorer OL 5. Park by St. Peter's church at the foot of Hallin Fell (GR 436193) and follow the road S to Martindale old church. Take AW's route up to Steel Knotts and his ridge routes to Wether Hill (1 hour 30), Loadpot Hill (1 hour 50), Bonscale Pike (2 hours 20) and Arthur's Pike (2 hours 35). Descend NE by the path which passes White Knott on your left and eventually joins the Howtown path. Follow this SW to Mellguards (GR 446196). Cross Fusedale Beck and take the path W round the foot of Steel End and so back to St. Peter's church.

10.5 miles/17 kms. 2,445ft/745m ascent. 4 hours.

20. Ard Crags - Knott Rigg (North-Western Fells).

O.S. Explorer OL 4. Park beside the Braithwaite to Buttermere road above Uzzicar (GR 233218). Walk S along the road to the Rigg Beck bridge (GR 229202). Follow AW's route of ascent via Aikin Knott to Ard Crags and his ridge route to Knott Rigg. Descend by reversing his route of ascent from Newlands Hause. Walk back along the road to the car.

8.5 miles/13.5 kms. 1,560ft/475m ascent. 3 hours 30.

21. Great Mell Fell (Eastern Fells).

O.S. Explorer OL 5. Limited parking where a track heads W (GR 407246), a little N of Brownrigg Farm. Follow the track till the second stile on your right. Cross it and follow the path SW then W by a field boundary till a path on your right climbs steeply NW. When this path peters out, follow the incline through Scots pine to the summit. Return by the same route. No trespass is involved.

2.25 miles/3.75 kms. 890ft/270m ascent. 2 hours.

N.B. If required, Great Mell Fell can easily be incorporated into route 16 above.

22. Great Crag (Central Fells).

O.S. Explorer OL 4. Start from Rosthwaite (GR 257148). Take the path NE towards Watendlath, but two-thirds of the way there (GR 268159) turn off right through a kissing-gate to join a clear path SSE. In due course this is diverted E to protect wetland and joins AW's route of ascent from Watendlath. Follow this to the summit. Return to Rosthwaite by the same route.

4 miles/6.5 kms. 1,115ft/340m ascent. 2 hours 5.

N.B. Weather and time permitting, Great Crag goes hand in hand with Grange Fell. See route 15 above.

Appendix

23. Fellbarrow - Low Fell (Western Fells).

O.S. Explorer OL 4. Limited roadside parking just N of Thackthwaite (GR 148237). Take AW's direct route A from Thackthwaite up Fellbarrow and his ridge route to Low Fell. Descend to Thackthwaite by reversing his ascent of Low Fell.

5 miles/8 kms. 1,430ft/435m ascent. 2 hours 30.

24. High Rigg - Raven Crag - High Tove - Armboth Fell (Central Fells).

O.S. Explorer OL 4 and 5. Limited roadside parking at Wanthwaite Bridge (GR 315232). Take the path beside St. John's Beck to Bridge House (GR 310227) and from there the path up to the church of St. John's-in-the-Vale (GR 306225). Follow AW's route up High Rigg and descend by the long southern ridge, joining St. John's Beck where it is crossed by the A591. Turn left along the road and first right onto a minor road over the Thirlmere dam. At the junction turn right and follow AW's route up Raven Crag (2 hours 10). Return to the main forestry track below the summit, turn left and follow it till a gate on your right allows access onto the open fell (GR 298182). Head SW across marsh and heather to join the fence at Eddy Grave Stake (GR 290170). Follow the fence W then S to High Tove. Continue S by the fence, eventually swinging E using any higher ground to avoid the worst of the marsh, and so to Armboth Fell (GR 297159; 4 hours 30). Descend N, crossing Fisher Gill to join the path from High Tove to Armboth. Turn right and descend to the Thirlmere road. Turn left along the road. At the junction with the dam road keep straight on. Where the plantation on your left ends, a track leads to Shoulthwaite Farm (GR 299204). From here cross the A591 and take the path N by

Shaw Bank (GR 303215). It leads into a minor road heading N and then a track heading E back to the church of St. John's-in-the-Vale. Return to Wanthwaite Bridge by your outward route.

14.75 miles/23.5 kms. 2,125ft/645m ascent. 7 hours 10.

25. Steel Fell - Calf Crag - Gibson Knott - Helm Crag (Central Fells).

O.S. Explorer OL 5 and 7. Start from Grasmere. Follow AW's ascent of Steel Fell (1 hour) and his ridge routes to Calf Crag (1 hour 40), Gibson Knott (2 hours 25) and Helm Crag (2 hours 55). Descend to Grasmere by reversing his ascent of Helm Crag.

8.5 miles/13.5 kms. 2,405ft/730m ascent. 4 hours 15.

Chapter Seven

26. Wetherlam - Swirl How - Great Carrs - Grey Friar - Dow Crag - Brim Fell - Coniston Old Man (Southern Fells).

O.S. Explorer OL 6. Start from Coniston. Take the path beside the Sun Inn and follow AW's route of ascent via Red Dell to Wetherlam (1 hour 50) and his ridge routes to Swirl How (2 hours 50), Great Carrs (3 hours 5) and Grey Friar (3 hours 30). Return towards Great Carrs but veer SSE then S on a path which contours round below Brim Fell to Goat's Hause (GR 266984). Take the path W then S to Dow Crag (5 hours). Return to Goat's Hause and climb steeply ENE till the path divides, at which point bear left to Brim Fell (5 hours 35). Follow AW's ridge route to Coniston Old Man (5 hours 55). Descend to Coniston by reversing his direct route of ascent, passing through the old mine workings and taking the path by Church Beck, which leads to the Sun Inn.

12 miles/19.25 kms. 4,325ft/1,320m ascent. 7 hours 30.

27. Lank Rigg - Crag Fell - Grike (Western Fells).

O.S. Explorer OL 4. Park beside the minor road below Blakeley Raise (GR 067130) and take the track heading E. This is the start of AW's route of ascent from the Coldfell road up to Lank Rigg (1 hour 25. I could not find the path which, according to AW, passes round the western flank of Whoap to the col.

Instead I climbed to the top of Whoap, from where the path down to the col and up Lank Rigg is clear). Return to the top of Whoap and descend NE over pathless moorland to the wall which runs NW from Caw Fell to the foot of Crag Fell. Follow the wall into the plantation where a good path leads directly to Crag Fell (2 hours 40). Take AW's ridge route to Grike (3 hours 10). Descend SW to the forestry track and follow it W to the road at Scaly Moss (GR 062137). Turn left along the road to the car.

8 miles/13 kms. 2,240ft/685m ascent. 4 hours 10.

28. Lingmell - Scafell Pike - Great End - Seathwaite Fell (Southern Fells).

O.S. Explorer OL 4 and 6. Park at Seathwaite (GR 235123). Follow AW's ascent of Scafell Pike from Borrowdale via Sty Head and the Corridor route as far as the Lingmell col. Here turn right (NW) and climb straight up the grassy slope to Lingmell (2 hours 15). Return to the col and rejoin the well-worn path up to Scafell Pike (3 hours 5). Follow AW's ridge route to Great End (4 hours). Rejoin the Esk Hause path and descend by Esk Hause to Sprinkling Tarn (GR 227092). Here leave the Sty Head path and go N in search of the summit of Seathwaite Fell and the cairn above Aaron Crags (5 hours 45). Descend the NW flank of Seathwaite Fell (no path), avoiding the crags, to the Sty Head path and so back to Seathwaite.

11 miles/17.5 kms. 3, 750ft/1,140m ascent. 7 hours.

29. Bleaberry Fell - High Seat (Central Fells).

O.S. Explorer OL 4. Limited roadside parking near Castlerigg Farm on the minor road to Rakefoot (GR 283226). Walk to the road end, leaving Rakefoot on your left. Follow the path up beside the wall, passing Walla Crag on your right. Join the path which climbs SE to the sheepfold (GR 278201) and so to the summit of Bleaberry Fell (1 hour). Follow AW's ridge route to High Seat (1 hour 30). Return by your outward route.

7.5 miles/12 kms. 1,340ft/410m ascent. 3 hours 5.

30. Catstycam - Birkhouse Moor (Eastern Fells).

O.S. Explorer OL 5. Start from Patterdale. Walk along the road to Glenridding. Immediately before Glenridding Beck turn left up to Gillside and Miresbeck (GR 378167). Here climb steeply beside the wall on your right and join the path which contours NW then SW above Glenridding Beck to the sheepfold (GR 357168). From here follow AW's ascent of Catstycam via Redtarn Beck and the east shoulder to the summit (2 hours 20). Descend SW towards Swirral Edge, turning left down to Red Tarn at the depression. Follow the path E then NE to Birkhouse Moor (4 hours). Descend to Glenridding by way of Mires Beck (see AW's ascent from Glenridding) and so to Patterdale.

9.5 miles/15 kms. 2,610ft/785m ascent. 5 hours 30.

Doing the Wainwrights

31. Sheffield Pike - Glenridding Dodd
(Eastern Fells).

O.S. Explorer OL 5. Limited parking at Dockray (GR 394216). Take the track by the telephone kiosk onto Watermillock Common. Here a path meanders SW, eventually joining a wall which comes in from the E. The path follows the wall below Swineside Knott (GR 379197) before climbing away from it to cross another wall below Brown Hills (GR 372193). Follow the path round Glencoyne Head before descending over grass to the depression at Nick Head (GR 364184). Take the path straight up the incline ahead to Sheffield Pike (1 hour 40). Return to Nick Head and turn right down towards Glencoyne. On reaching the western edge of Glencoyne Wood, leave the path and follow the wall S below Heron Pike (tough going when the bracken is high). Where the wall is crossed by another at right-angles (GR 377175), turn left and climb easily onto Glenridding Dodd (3 hours). Descend to the A592 by way of Mossdale Beck (the path starts well but soon peters out in a jungle of head-high bracken). Turn left along the road to the junction with the A5091 (if cattle do not bother you, a footpath cuts across Glencoyne Park from one road to the other at GR 393194) and so back to Dockray.

9.25 miles/14.75 kms. 1,565ft/475m ascent. 5 hours 20.

N.B. This route was dictated by thick mist on Sheffield Pike. A much better way onto Glenridding Dodd is to continue SE over Sheffield Pike to Heron Pike and then descend the SE ridge to the wall which leads onto Glenridding Dodd.

Appendix

32. Esk Pike - Bowfell - Rossett Pike (Southern Fells).

O.S. Explorer OL 4 and 6. Park at Seathwaite (GR 235123). Follow AW's ascent of Esk Pike from Borrowdale (1 hour 45) and his ridge route to Bowfell (2 hours 25). Return towards Esk Pike but, at Ore Gap (GR 241073), turn right down to Angle Tarn. Follow the Langdale path SE before turning left (E) onto Rossett Pike (4 hours 20). Return to Angle Tarn and climb on a good path NW past Allen Crags till you rejoin the Esk Hause - Seathwaite path and so back to Seathwaite.

10 miles/16 kms. 3,585ft/1,090m ascent. 6 hours 50.

Chapter Eight

33a. Hard Knott (Southern Fells).

O.S. Explorer OL 6. Limited parking at the top of Hardknott Pass (GR 233015). Take AW's route of ascent to the summit (30 minutes) and return by the same route. Note that the scree-run of which he speaks is now by-passed and a new fence marks the line of ascent and descent clearly.

0.75 mile/1.2 kms. 550ft/165m ascent. 55 minutes.

33b. Slight Side - Scafell (Southern Fells).

O.S. Explorer OL 6. Limited roadside parking W of Whahouse Bridge (GR 204008). Follow AW's ascent of Slight Side from Eskdale (1 hour 45) and his ridge route to Scafell (2 hours 40). Return by the same route.

9 miles/14.5 kms. 3,100ft/945m ascent. 5 hours 40.

34. Grisedale Pike - Hopegill Head - Whiteside (North-Western Fells).

O.S. Explorer OL 4. Car-park NW of Braithwaite (GR 226242). Take AW's route from Braithwaite up Grisedale Pike (1 hour 20; the path starts from the car-park). Follow his ridge routes to Hopegill Head (1 hour 55) and Whiteside (2 hours 20). Return to Hopegill Head by the same route and descend over Sand Hill

Appendix

to Coledale Hause (GR 188213). Return to Braithwaite by the track which follows Coledale Beck.

10.5 miles/17 kms. 3,300ft/1,005m ascent. 4 hours 45.

Chapter Nine

35a. Green Crag - Harter Fell (Southern Fells).

O.S. Explorer OL 6. Limited roadside parking near the Woolpack Inn (GR 191010). Follow AW's route from Eskdale via Low Birker to Green Crag (1 hour 10). Descend by his alternative route, passing to the E of Crook Crag and joining the Harter Fell path below Kepple Crag. Turn right and follow his route of ascent from Eskdale till almost at the foot of the Harter Fell crags. Here turn right along a path which contours round Harter Fell before climbing steeply but easily from the SE, on a good path from the Duddon valley, up to the summit (3 hours 15). Make the direct descent W, reversing AW's route of ascent, and so back to the Woolpack Inn via Penny Hill Farm.

9 miles/14.5 kms. 2,850ft/870m ascent. 4 hours 45.

35b. Whin Rigg - Illgill Head (Southern Fells).

O.S. Explorer OL 6. Off-road parking at the foot of Irton Pike (GR 123013). Take the forestry track signposted 'Public Footpath Wasdale Head'. Disregard tracks branching off left and come out onto open pasture (very muddy when wet). The path heads NE and improves greatly once over the first wall, from where it is clearly visible all the way to Whin Rigg (1 hour). Follow the escarpment above Wast Water NE to Illgill Head (1 hour 55 - a lot of photographs to be taken!). Return by the same route.

7.5 miles/12 kms. 2,100ft/640m ascent. 3 hours 35.

36. Dodd - Carl Side - Long Side - Ullock Pike (Northern Fells).

O.S. Explorer OL 4. Car-park at Mirehouse (GR 235282). Take the metalled forestry road just N of the car-park and climb through the forest on the N side of Skill Beck. In due course the road becomes a stony track, bears to the right and joins a major Forestry Commission track, from which the track to Dodd (signposted) branches off on the right (GR 250274). From the summit (55 minutes) return to the signposted junction and turn right along the main track and almost immediately left onto a path which climbs up to White Stones (GR 254273). Here turn left up the path to Carl Side (1 hour 45). Follow AW's ridge routes to Long Side and Ullock Pike (2 hours 25). Descend by reversing his ascent from Ravenstone (GR 236297). From here a footpath just inside the wood skirts the A591 all the way to the Mirehouse car-park.

7.5 miles/12 kms. 2,665ft/810m ascent. 3 hours 30.

37. Red Pike (Buttermere) - High Stile - High Crag - Haystacks - Fleetwith Pike (Western Fells).

O.S. Explorer OL 4. Catch the bus from Keswick to Buttermere. Follow AW's route up Red Pike via Scale Force (I followed the beck to the tributary and turned left, but the earlier turn-off through heather makes a better route). From Red Pike (2 hours 5) follow AW's ridge routes to High Stile (2 hours 30), High Crag (3 hours 25 after a lunch-stop; beware of making for

Grey Crags by mistake) and Haystacks (4 hours 30). Take the path ESE round the head of Warnscale Beck, cross the stream and continue E before striking off NNW across rough grassland to the summit of Fleetwith Pike (5 hours 45. This is hard work - better is to continue E to the ridge above Honister where a good path climbs NW to the summit). Descend SE by the ridge path to the dismantled tramway at Drum House (GR 216135) and turn left down to Honister Hause (6 hours 35). Walk down the road to Seatoller and catch the bus to Keswick.

12 miles/19.25 kms. 3,890ft/1,185m ascent. 7 hours 5.

38. Knott - Great Calva (Northern Fells).

O.S. Explorer OL 4 and 5. Park just beyond the bridge over Grainsgill Beck (GR 327327). Take the track NW through the old mine workings to the bothy (GR 313336) on Great Lingy Hill. Turn left along a path which crosses Grainsgill Beck at GR 311333 (an alternative is to start by climbing up Grainsgill Beck to this point). The path continues all the way to the summit of Knott (1 hour 10), keeping just below and to the N of the ridge running W from Coomb Height. From Knott follow AW's ridge route to Great Calva (1 hour 55). Descend to Wiley Gill by the fence which runs E from the lower cairn. A footbridge (GR 302307) gives access to the Mosedale track. Follow this NE back to the car.

7.5 miles/12 kms. 1,860ft/560m ascent. 3 hours 30.

N.B. For those with fresher legs than mine were, it is possible to combine this route with that over Carrock Fell and High Pike (see route 49 below), in which case start from Mosedale (GR 357323). Walk N along the road towards Calebreck, then follow route 49 to the summit of High Pike, at which point retrace your steps SW and continue in that direction to the bothy on Great Lingy Hill. From there follow the route given above and return to Mosedale by the road.

39. Tarn Crag (Central Fells).

O.S. Explorer OL 6 and 7. Start from Grasmere. Take the Easedale road and the path via Sour Milk Gill to Easedale Tarn (1 hour 5). Here I made my way round the northern side of the tarn (no clear path) before rejoining the path to Belles Knott: it is much better to keep to the path on the south side of the Tarn. Just beyond Belles Knott a path heads NE, passing along the eastern side of Codale Tarn and leading eventually to the summit of Tarn Crag (2 hours 20). Return to Grasmere by the same route.

7.75 miles/12.5 kms. 1,600ft/490m ascent. 4 hours 35.

N.B. My plan had been to climb Tarn Crag by the east ridge as described by AW, but I missed the turning over Sour Milk Gill. Those with sharper eyes than mine can make a round of it by going up the east ridge and descending by the route described above.

Chapter Ten

40. Lonscale Fell - Skiddaw Little Man - Skiddaw - Bakestall (Northern Fells).

O.S. Explorer OL 4 and 5. Start from Threlkeld. Walk W to the junction with the A66 (GR 316248) and take the footpath W along the disused railway line. Shortly after crossing the River Greta for the fourth time (GR 298247), turn right across a field and left up a part-metalled road past Brundholme. At a stile (GR 296252) leave the road for a track which climbs W up the brow of the hill to the Gale Road car-park (GR 282254). From here ascend Lonscale Fell (1 hour 40) by AW's route A from Keswick. Follow his ridge routes to Skiddaw Little Man (2 hours 30, after attempting to watch a fell race en route), Skiddaw (2 hours 50) and Bakestall. Follow the fence NE down to the track at Whitewater Dash (GR 273314; 3 hours 35) and turn right along it, passing Skiddaw House and skirting the eastern and southern flanks of Lonscale Fell and so back to the Gale Road car-park. Return to Threlkeld by your outward route.

15.75 miles/25 kms. 3,105ft/945m ascent. 6 hours 25.

N.B. If it has not been climbed already, it is a simple matter to visit Latrigg from the Gale Road car-park by walking SSW up the path to the summit. Descend the eastern slope till the path joins a minor road at a stile (GR 296252), thus rejoining the route described above.

Appendix

41. Hart Side - Stybarrow Dodd - Watson's Dodd - Great Dodd (Eastern Fells).

O.S. Explorer OL 5. Car-park at the eastern end of the Old Coach Road (GR 380219). Walk down the metalled road to Dowthwaitehead. Turn S over a footbridge and follow the former miners' track SSW. At a gate, take the upper path on your right which leads eventually to a stile in a stone wall (GR 369194). A path on the far side follows the wall up before finally veering W to the summit of Birkett Fell. From here a path heads due W to Hart Side (1 hour 30). Follow AW's ridge routes to Stybarrow Dodd (2 hours 10), Watson's Dodd (2 hours 25) and Great Dodd (3 hours 5). Descend by reversing his route of ascent from Dockray via Groove Beck (some widely spaced cairns on the northern side of Great Dodd lead into the path which swings NE over Randerside).

9.75 miles/15.5 kms. 2,005ft/610m ascent. 4 hours.

42a. Yewbarrow (Western Fells).

O.S. Explorer OL 6. Car-park at Overbeck Bridge (GR 167068). Follow AW's route of ascent from here (1 hour 10). Continue NNE to the depression where a path slants down on your left, thus avoiding Stirrup Crag. Drop down to the path (easier said than done) which follows Over Beck back to Overbeck Bridge.

3.5 miles/5.5 kms. 1,900ft/580m ascent. 3 hours.

42b. Middle Fell - Seatallan - Buckbarrow (Western Fells).

O.S. Explorer OL 6. Limited roadside parking at Greendale (GR 145056). Follow AW's ascent of Middle Fell from here (1 hour) and his ridge route to Seatallan (2 hours 5). A path leads down to Buckbarrow (2 hours 55) by way of Cat Bields (GR 132069) and Glade How. Return to Greendale by reversing AW's ascent of Buckbarrow.

6.75 miles/11 kms. 2,380ft/725m ascent. 3 hours 55.

43. Holme Fell - Black Fell (Southern Fells).

O.S. Explorer OL 7. Park at Tom Gill car-park (GR 323998). Walk about 200 metres W along the A593 to Yew Tree Farm, where a footpath leads by way of Uskdale Gap to Holme Fell (50 minutes; see AW's map of Holme Fell). Descend to the A593 at Oxen Fell (1 hour 50) by the route illustrated by AW. Cross the road and follow the lane leading SE to Borwick Lodge. At a signposted gate (GR 336006) turn left and climb through Iron Keld plantation before turning right on a good path to Black Fell (3 hours 15). Return by the same route to that point on the Borwick Lodge lane (GR 332007) where the Cumbria Way turns off left (S) to Tarn Hows. Walk round the E and S sides of Tarn Hows and return to Tom Gill car-park by the path (GR 327997) which follows the stream NW then W from Tarn Hows.

7.25 miles/11.5 kms. 1,280ft/390m ascent. 4 hours 50.

44. Burnbank Fell - Blake Fell - Gavel Fell - Great Borne - Starling Dodd (Western Fells).

O.S. Explorer OL 4. Car-park at Maggie's Bridge (GR 135210). Take the track to the head of Loweswater and climb through Holme Wood on a path slanting W to emerge just above Holme Beck (GR 118213). Cross the beck and follow it upstream before climbing steeply NW onto the shoulder of Burnbank Fell. From the summit (1 hour 10), follow AW's ridge routes to Blake Fell (1 hour 30) and Gavel Fell (1 hour 55). Follow the fence S, turning left at a T-junction of fences well before the Flautern Pass (GR 121173; very boggy in places) and stay with this fence all the way to the top of Great Borne (2 hours 50). Follow AW's ridge route to Starling Dodd (3 hours 40). Descend to the head of Scale Beck and follow it down to Scale Force (4 hours 35. This is a laborious route - better is to make for Lingcomb Edge and take that path down to Scale Force). Follow the path which runs NW then N into Mosedale (avoid heading W on the Flautern Pass) and so back to Loweswater and Maggie's Bridge.

11.25 miles/18 kms. 3,175ft/965m ascent. 5 hours 55.

Chapter Twelve

45. Silver How - Blea Rigg - Sergeant Man - Pavey Ark (Central Fells).

O.S. Explorer OL 6 and 7. Start from Grasmere. Take the more easterly of AW's routes from Grasmere to Silver How (1 hour 5) by way of the Chapel Stile path. Follow his ridge routes to Blea Rigg (2 hours 20) and Sergeant Man (3 hours 15). Take the path W then S, leaving Thunacar Knott on your right as you branch off left on a path (GR 279083) which runs SE to Pavey Ark (3 hours 55; the summit is hard to find in poor conditions). Return to Silver How by your outward route (6 hours 30). Descend to Grasmere by way of Wray Gill, crossing it on a path (GR 325073) which leads down to Allan Bank and so to Grasmere.

12.5 miles/20 kms. 2,915ft/890m ascent. 7 hours 20.

46. Pike o'Blisco - Cold Pike - Crinkle Crags (Southern Fells).

O.S. Explorer OL 6. Use one of the Great Langdale car-parks. Take AW's route of ascent from Dungeon Ghyll via Wall End to Pike o'Blisco (2 hours). Follow his ridge routes to Cold Pike (2 hours 45) and Crinkle Crags (4 hours 10 to the top of the second Crinkle). Descend to Dungeon Ghyll by reversing his route of ascent via The Band and Three Tarns, and so back to the car.

12 miles/19 kms. 3,850ft/1,175m ascent. 6 hours 50.

47. Harrison Stickle - Pike o'Stickle - Loft Crag (Central Fells) + Lingmoor Fell (Southern Fells).

O.S. Explorer OL 6 and 7. Limited roadside parking on the B5343 W of Chapel Stile. Take the track (GR 312063) which keeps to the N of Great Langdale Beck and leads to the New Dungeon Ghyll car-park. From the New Hotel take AW's route of ascent via Pike How to Harrison Stickle (1 hour 45). Follow his ridge routes to Pike o'Stickle (2 hours 25) and Loft Crag (2 hours 40). Descend by reversing his easternmost route of ascent from Dungeon Ghyll, eventually taking the path by the wall W to the Old Hotel (4 hours 15). Follow his route up Lingmoor Fell (5 hours 25), skirting the southern flank of Side Pike by way of a path (GR 294052) which leaves the road about a quarter of a mile beyond the point indicated by AW. Return to the Old Hotel by your outward route and so back to the car.

10 miles/16 kms. 3,680ft/1,120m ascent. 6 hours 55.

48a. Sallows - Sour Howes (Far Eastern Fells).

O.S. Explorer OL 7. Limited parking by Trout Beck just W of Church Bridge (GR 414027). Walk 200 metres S along the A592 and take the track on the left, the Garburn Road, which climbs up to the Garburn Pass. Here turn right at the second gate (there is a stile) and follow a path S then E to Sallows (1 hour 10). From here a path leads W to a stone wall with a stile. Cross this and take the path which follows the wall S before veering away SW to Sour Howes (1 hour 45. In mist Sour Howes may be easily by-passed. If you reach a wall running NE/SW you have gone too far and must turn back). Return to the Garburn

Pass by your outward path, but this time keep the wall on your right till you are almost at the Pass. Return to Church Bridge by your outward route.

6.25 miles/10 kms. 1,345ft/410m ascent. 2 hours 55.

48b. Wansfell (Far Eastern Fells).

O.S. Explorer OL 7. From Church Bridge take the minor road W to a T-junction and turn right, up to Troutbeck. Turn left along Nanny Lane (sign-posted). In due course the track becomes a path which soon crosses the wall on your left. It then follows the line of the wall and leads eventually to Wansfell (55 minutes). From here a clear path leads SW over frequently boggy ground to Wansfell Pike (1 hour 25). A good path runs E to join Nanny Lane at a gate and so back to Church Bridge.

5.25 miles/8.5 kms. 1,265 ft/385m ascent. 2 hours 15.

Chapter Thirteen

49. Carrock Fell - High Pike (Northern Fells).

O.S. Explorer OL 5. Roadside parking just N of Stone Ends (GR 354337). Follow AW's route of ascent from Stone Ends up to Carrock Fell (45 minutes) and his ridge route to High Pike (1 hour 25). Descend by reversing his route of ascent from Calebrack by way of Driggeth Mine, but keep to the track till it joins the Mosedale road near Carrock Beck. Turn right and walk back to the car.

6.5 miles/10.5 kms. 1,730ft/525m ascent. 2 hours 25.

50. Raise - White Side - Helvellyn - Nethermost Pike - Dollywaggon Pike (Eastern Fells).

O.S. Explorer OL 5. Start from Patterdale. Walk to Glenridding village and take the Greenside road N of Glenridding Beck to the Youth Hostel. From here follow AW's route of ascent via the disused aqueduct to Raise (1 hour 55) and his ridge routes to White Side (2 hours 20) and Helvellyn Lower Man. Continue S till the path from Thirlspot comes in from the NW and follow it SE to Helvellyn (2 hours 55). Take AW's ridge routes to Nethermost Pike (3 hours 25. It is easy to by-pass this in mist - if you start descending, retrace your steps) and Dollywaggon Pike (3 hours 55). Descend to Grisedale Tarn and walk down Grisedale to Grisedale Bridge (GR 391163) and so back to Patterdale.

14 miles/22.5 kms. 3,450ft/1,050m ascent. 6 hours 10.

51. Angletarn Pikes - Brock Crags - The Nab - Rest Dodd - The Knott (Far Eastern Fells).

O.S. Explorer OL 5. Limited parking at Deepdale Bridge (GR 399144). Take the path E over fields to join the Rooking - Hartsop path after crossing Goldrill Beck. At the junction turn right, then left to climb up to Boardale Hause. Here take the path on your right, passing to the W of Stony Rigg and so to Angletarn Pikes (1 hour 5). Rejoin the path which passes below Angletarn Pikes and follow it alongside Angle Tarn to Satura Crag. Here (GR 423137) turn right and follow the wall W to Brock Crags (1 hour 55). Return to Satura Crag and continue E on a path which climbs over the western flank of Rest Dodd and joins a wall running W to E. Follow this E to a stile (GR 435141), cross the wall and take the path N over boggy ground to The Nab (2 hours 55). Return to the stile, cross the wall and continue straight ahead up a very steep path to Rest Dodd (3 hours 25). Follow AW's ridge route to The Knott (4 hours 15). Descend to the Patterdale path and follow it back to Boardale Hause and so to Deepdale Bridge.

11 miles/17.5 kms. 3,230ft/985m ascent. 6 hours 25.

52. Causey Pike - Scar Crags - Sail - Outerside - Barrow (North-Western Fells).

O.S. Explorer OL 4. Start from Braithwaite. Walk along the Buttermere road until the track to Sail Pass by way of Stonycroft Gill leaves the road on your right above Uzzicar (GR 233217). Follow this track up to High Moss, where a path on your left cuts obliquely up to Causey Pike (1 hour 40). Follow AW's ridge routes to Scar Crags (2 hours 15) and Sail (2 hours 40). Return to Sail Pass and turn left down the track to High Moss. Here leave the track and make directly for Outerside over very wet ground, climbing to the summit (4 hours) from the W. Retrace your steps to rejoin the track and follow it down by Stonycroft Gill, before turning off left on a good path (GR 218216) which crosses the summit of Barrow (4 hours 55) and continues all the way to Braithwaite.

9.5 miles/15 kms. 3,055ft/930m ascent. 5 hours 30.

Chapter Fifteen

53. Troutbeck Tongue - Froswick - Ill Bell - Yoke (Far Eastern Fells).

O.S. Explorer OL 7. Limited parking by Trout Beck just W of Church Bridge (GR 414027). Take the minor road W to a T-junction and turn right, following the road through Troutbeck to the junction with the A592 at Town Head. Cross the A592 and follow Ing Lane N to Hagg Bridge (GR 423055). Bear right across fields before making a direct ascent of Troutbeck Tongue (1 hour 20). Walk NNE the length of the Tongue and join the path which climbs steeply towards Thornthwaite Crag. In due course cut off E to join the path which runs from High Street all the way to the Garburn Pass. Turn right and follow it over Froswick (2 hours 25) and Ill Bell (2 hours 50) to Yoke (3 hours 25) - see AW's ridge routes to Ill Bell and Yoke. Descend to the Garburn Pass (4 hours 5) by reversing AW's route up Yoke and follow the Garburn Road (a track) back to the A592 and so to Chuch Bridge.

10 miles/16 kms. 3,115ft/950m ascent. 4 hours 50.

54. Robinson - Hindscarth - Dale Head - High Spy - Maiden Moor - Catbells (North-Western Fells).

O.S. Explorer OL 4. Limited parking near the foot of Catbells (GR 247213). Follow the track on the W side of Catbells to Skelgill and Little Town. Take the metalled road to Newlands

Church (GR 230194). From here follow AW's route via High Snab Bank to Robinson (1 hour 50). Take the path S then SE to Littledale Edge where a path, new since Wainwright's day, leads NE directly to the summit of Hindscarth (2 hours 20). Follow AW's ridge routes to Dale Head (2 hours 45), High Spy (3 hours 35), Maiden Moor (4 hours 5) and Catbells (4 hours 35). Descend to the Skelgill - Little Town track by a path which cuts obliquely down the W flank of Catbells and so back to the car.

13 miles/21 kms. 3,810ft/1,160m ascent. 5 hours 10
(done in a hurry without a lunch-stop).

55. Grey Knotts - Brandreth (Western Fells).

O.S. Explorer OL 4. Start from Grange (GR 253175). Take the track SW passing Castle Crag on your left. At a junction shortly before Seatoller (GR 244143) bear right to Little Gatesgarthdale and continue up the road to Honister Hause (1 hour 20). Follow AW's direct route of ascent by the fence to Grey Knotts (2 hours 20) and his ridge route to Brandreth (2 hours 35). Return to Honister Hause (3 hours 30) by reversing his route from there up to Brandreth. Return to Grange by your outward route.

10.25 miles/16.5 kms. 2,045ft/615m ascent. 5 hours 15.

N.B. When the roads are not icy, Honister Hause is a more logical starting-point for this route, in which case it will take just 2 hours 10 minutes, making it reasonable to incorporate Green Gable, Great Gable and Kirk Fell into this excursion: see route 60 below.

Chapter Sixteen

56a. Stone Arthur (Eastern Fells).

O.S. Explorer OL 7. Start from Grasmere. Follow AW's route of ascent from the Swan Hotel. Once on the open fell, it is possible to continue on the path which contours round above Greenhead Gill before turning NW to Stone Arthur (1 hour. Take care not to by-pass Stone Arthur on your left). Return to Grasmere by the same route.

2.5 miles/4 kms. 1,405ft/430m ascent. 1 hour 50.

56b. Loughrigg Fell (Central Fells).

O.S. Explorer OL 7. Follow AW's route of ascent from Grasmere to the summit (1 hour). Using the network of paths, descend NE to join the main Grasmere-Rydal path above Rydal Water. Here turn left and, on reaching woodland, turn right, descending through the trees to a footbridge (GR 347064) over the River Rothay. Continue to the A591, cross it and take the minor road back to Grasmere via How Top (GR 344067) and Dove Cottage.

5.25 miles/8.5 kms. 920ft/280m ascent. 2 hours 25.

57. Grasmoor - Eel Crag - Wandope - Whiteless Pike - Rannerdale Knotts (North-Western Fells).

O.S. Explorer OL 4. Park at Cinderdale Common (GR 163194). Take AW's route of ascent from Rannerdale via Lad Hows to Grasmoor (1 hour 25) and his ridge routes to Eel Crag (1 hour 55), Wandope (2 hours 10) and Whiteless Pike (2 hours 35). Descend by reversing his route of ascent from Buttermere, but at the col after Whiteless Breast turn right (NW) on a good path over Low Bank to Rannerdale Knotts (4 hours). Descend to the Buttermere road by a very steep path W (AW's ascent from Rannerdale depicts most of this path clearly, but the start from the summit must be sought). Turn right along the road to Cinderdale Common.

7.25 miles/11.5 kms. 3,330ft/1,015m ascent. 4 hours 50.

58. Base Brown - Green Gable (Western Fells).

O.S. Explorer OL 4. Park at Seathwaite (GR 235123). Follow AW's route of ascent passing below the Hanging Stone to reach Base Brown (1 hour 15). Continue by his ridge route to Green Gable (1 hour 50). Return by reversing his route of ascent from Seathwaite.

4.75 miles/7.5 kms. 2,395ft/730m ascent. 3 hours 30.

N.B. Had the conditions permitted, I would have continued over Great Gable and, possibly, Kirk Fell, which would have made a full day's excursion.

59a. High Hartsop Dodd (Eastern Fells).

O.S. Explorer OL 5. Car-park at Cow Bridge (GR 403134). Take the track to Hartsop Hall (GR 398121). From here follow AW's route up High Hartsopp Dodd (1 hour). Return by the same route.

3.5 miles/5.5 kms. 1,180ft/360m ascent. 1 hour 55.

N.B. This out-and-back route was dictated by the conditions. Normally High Hartsopp Dodd would be part of a round including Little Hart Crag, Red Screes and Middle Dodd: see route 61 below.

59b. Hartsop above How (Eastern Fells).

O.S. Explorer OL 5. Take the footpath N from Cow Bridge through Low Wood. Shortly after you join the A592, a gate on your left gives access to Deepdale Park. From here, follow AW's route up Hartsop above How (1 hour 5). Return by the same route.

5 miles/8 kms. 1,435ft/435m ascent. 2 hours 30.

N.B. This out-and-back route is an inevitable mopping-up operation after the Fairfield horseshoe.

Chapter Seventeen

60. Great Gable - Kirk Fell (Western Fells).

O.S. Explorer OL 4. Start from Honister Hause (GR 225135). Follow AW's route of ascent from Honister Pass to Great Gable, but note that the fence which leads up to Brandreth must be followed higher than AW shows before a path veers off S to Stone Cove. From the summit of Great Gable (2 hours) return to Stone Cove and turn left on a path which leads W to Beck Head (GR 205107). From here follow the fence posts over Rib End and the lower summit of Kirk Fell to the true summit (3 hours 25) - see the latter part of AW's ridge route from Great Gable to Kirk Fell. Return to Stone Cove and rejoin your outward route and so back to Honister Hause.

8.25 miles/13 kms. 2,650ft/805m ascent. 5 hours 20 (without any stops en route).

61. Little Hart Crag - Red Screes - Middle Dodd (Eastern Fells).

O.S. Explorer OL 5 and 7. Car-park at Cow Bridge (GR 403134). Take the track S to Hartsop Hall (GR 398121). Continue S up Caiston Glen to Scandale Pass (GR 388096). Turn right and follow the path up to Little Hart Crag (1 hour 30). Take AW's ridge route to Red Screes (2 hours 30), descend over Middle Dodd by reversing his route up Red Screes from Patterdale and so back to Cow Bridge. (Note that on Middle Dodd, after crossing the wall that runs east/west, there is a path which leads straight to the top of sheer crags. The wall to the west offers a safe line of descent, as illustrated by AW).

9.25 miles/15 kms. 2,600ft/790m ascent. 4 hours 40.

N.B. High Hartsop Dodd can easily be incorporated into this route, climbing it first and continuing up the ridge to Little Hart Crag. See route 59a.

62. Rampsgill Head - High Raise - Kidsty Pike - High Street - Mardale Ill Bell - Thornthwaite Crag - Gray Crag - Caudale Moor (or Stony Cove Pike) - Hartsop Dodd (Far Eastern Fells).

O.S. Explorer OL 5. Parking at Hartsop, beside Hayeswater Gill (GR 409132). Walk E up the track to Hayeswater, keeping to the S of Hayeswater Gill when the track divides. Cross over the footbridge and climb obliquely E then N to join the Patterdale-High Street path W of The Knott. Turn right along this and follow it round to the E side of The Knott, before leaving it to make straight for Rampsgill Head (1 hour 15). Follow AW's ridge route to High Raise (1 hour 35). Return to the depression, from where a path leads S to Kidsty Pike (1 hour 50). Head W on a path which rounds the Head of Riggindale and joins High Street, the Roman road. Follow this S to the summit of High Street (2 hours 30). Take AW's ridge routes to Mardale Ill Bell (3 hours), Thornthwaite Crag (3 hours 25 - a clear path all the way) and Gray Crag (3 hours 50). Return towards Thornthwaite Crag and, after passing the high point mid-way along the ridge, leave the path and head SSW, following the contours to join the Thornthwaite Crag-Stony Cove Pike path about 300 metres above the depression of Threshthwaite Mouth. Follow this path W to Stony Cove Pike/Caudale Moor (4 hours 50). Take AW's ridge route to Hartsop Dodd (5 hours 25). Make the direct descent down the steep N ridge, turning right at the first wall, and so back to Hartsop.

13 miles/21 kms. 3,840ft/1,170m ascent. 6 hours 15.

N.B. If this route seems excessively long, omit Stony Cove Pike and Hartsop Dodd and descend the N ridge of Gray Crag till a route E to the Hayeswater dam can be found. Return by the track to Hartsop (see AW's ascent of Gray Crag from Hartsop).

63. Seat Sandal (Eastern Fells).

O.S. Explorer OL 5 and 7. Start from Grasmere at the northern junction of the A591 and the B5287 (GR 339083). Follow AW's route of ascent from Grasmere, taking the more westerly path over Great Tongue on the way out and the path by Tongue Gill on the way back. 1 hour 40 to the summit.

6.25 miles/10 kms. 2,200ft/670m ascent. 3 hours 5.

64. Blencathra (Northern Fells).

O.S. Explorer OL 5. Park in the lay-by on the A66 opposite the White Horse Inn (GR 344268). Follow AW's route of ascent from Scales via Doddick Fell to the summit (1 hour 45). Retrace your steps to the top of Doddick Fell but continue E over Scales Fell to Mousthwaite Comb, joining the minor road near the bridge over Comb Beck (GR 348273). Turn right along the road to the White Horse Inn.

4.25 miles/7 kms. 2,150ft/645m ascent. 3 hours 55.

Doing the Wainwrights

N.B. This snail's rate of progress must be attributed to the icy conditions and the fact that a party invariably proceeds at a slower rate than an individual.

Index of Fells

For those fells with several entries, figures in bold indicate the main entries in the text and in the appendix.

Doing the Wainwrights

Index of Fells